W9-BSZ-460

The Modern Manuscript Library

by

Ruth B. Bordin and Robert M. Warner
Michigan Historical Collections
University of Michigan

The Scarecrow Press, Inc.
New York and London 1966

L.C. Card No. 66-13734

Table of Contents

Introduction

Manuscript libraries have been multiplying in the United States during the last two decades with extraordinary rapidity. Colleges and universities, governmental units, professional and scientific organizations, religious bodies and business firms are all busily starting libraries or archives in which manuscript materials are being accumulated. Much of the impetus for this rash of activity has probably come from the attention American society has focused on the great Presidential libraries. Certainly current interest in the planning for the Kennedy Library will not discourage the trend. Another stimulus has been the rapid expansion of higher education in the United States coupled with increased emphasis on using primary source material in the teaching of history. An expanded interest in regional, state and local history and the wider significance attached to its findings is also a factor.

Most rejoice that America is willing, and able, to provide such a rich variety of repositories for the safe-keeping of its significant written records. This proliferation of manuscript libraries and archives has resulted in the preservation of more of the nation's written records than at any other previous time in our history. More public and private funds are being spent for this purpose, and the number of individuals performing these services is constantly increasing. To cite but one example: in Michigan a decade ago there were only three publicly supported manuscript libraries, employing ten professionals. Today there are seven institutions employing twenty-six. This startling increase in the number of manuscript repositories plus modern methods of duplication and reproduction of records makes manuscript materials much more readily available to scholar and student.

However, this growth has also created problems. First of all, many of these new institutions are very different from their illustrious forerunners like the Clements, Newberry, or Bancroft libraries. Since most of the important documents and papers of past centuries have already found their way into institutional hands, the attention of newer institutions is focused either on more obscure materials or the very recent past. Both of these kinds of material are likely to run to bulk; the latter also needs great sensitivity in its handling. No longer is it the care and preservation of individual documents of great monetary value and considerable rarity that concerns the average manuscript librarian, but rather he is concerned with selecting from the great bulk of typewritten and mimeographed materials of the last generation those which really merit preservation.

The days are also passing when manuscript librarianship was a rare enough occupation so that its members could be recruited informally and could be either self-trained or could be taught the necessary skills by an apprentice system. American archival institutions faced up to this problem a generation ago, and the Society of American Archivists has contributed much to the professionalization of their craft. A literature has been accumulated, and formal training programs have been instituted. The archivists have filled the needs of manuscript libraries to some extent, but their problems are not identical and there are dangers in treating the two types of institutions as if their needs were interchangeable.

Just how does a manuscript library differ from an archive? Archives are the permanent records of a body, usually, but not necessarily, on-going, of either a public or private character. For example, units of government, churches and business firms create archives if their records are systematically disposed of in such a way that those of continuing administrative value or historical importance are preserved for future use by the body which created them, and only incidentally for the purposes of scholars. True a manuscript library can contain archives. Usually they will be of a non-ongoing body or placed there on deposit (rather than actually given) by some organization which does not have facilities for taking care of them itself. But these archival records are housed in a manuscript library only incidentally. They will form only a part of its total holdings. An archival institution will house records of a single body, albeit as vast as the federal government, and will exist only to preserve the records of that body. An archival institution's primary responsibility is to the agency which created the records and may have further use for them.

A manuscript library exists to serve the scholar and the student. It can devise its techniques to serve their purposes exclusively. Also while its scope may be drastically limited geographically, chronologically, or in some other way, it will rarely consist of the papers and records of a single institution. Its variety of materials, coming from a multiplicity of sources, will make its needs very different from those of an archival institution. There are great areas of commonality of course. Many of a manuscript library's materials will resemble or even be archival records. Many of the archivists' techniques will prove of value.

The books of Ernst Posner and T. R. Schellenberg have much to teach the manuscript librarian, but archival management is not synonymous with manuscript librarianship. Scattered articles in The American Archivist and more rarely in library journals could give the novice some assistance in formulating policies and developing techniques, but there has been no attempt anywhere to bring together in an organized fashion what manuscript librarianship is all about. What are the policies and problems that manuscript libraries have to evaluate and face? How do they accumulate materials? What techniques are available for handling their holdings? What obligations does the library have to its users? Anyone working in a manuscript library has to find answers to all these questions, but the process can be tortuous and solutions can be a long time in coming. It was to help in finding at least preliminary or partial answers to some of these questions that this book took shape. Generally the approach has been to pose practical rather than theoretical solutions although broad aspects of problems such as those related to contemporary records have been considered. This little volume raises as many problems as it answers and is not intended to present a definitive body of principles on which all manuscript libraries can be based. It is simply a first step which it is hoped will encourage others to offer further contributions in the field.

Acknowledgements

Since this book is primarily the outgrowth of our experience over the past decade at the Michigan Historical Collections of The University of Michigan, we are greatly indebted to this institution and our colleagues on the staff; particularly F. Clever Bald, Director, who encouraged our work and read all the chapters and to Sharon S. Doster who did most of the typing for us. Professor Russell E. Bidlack of The University of Michigan Department of Library Science contributed several valuable revisions of the manuscript and Professor Wallace J. Bonk of the same department assisted in arranging for its publication. Professor Philip P. Mason, University Archivist and Director of the Wayne State University Labor History Archives, read the entire manuscript and made many valuable suggestions for its improvement. All of these and other friends deserve our appreciation, but none may be blamed for any mistakes of fact or interpretation. We also acknowledge our thanks to *The American Archivist* for permission to quote from this basic publication and to the Library of Congress for permission to quote its rules for manuscript use.

Chapter I

Who Should Collect and What Should be Collected

A few decades ago the erection of a bell tower was the status symbol for the rising college or university. In the 1960's the status symbol tended to become the possession of a manuscript library or at least a college archive. Not only colleges but businesses, churches and government units in ever-increasing numbers are creating or expanding manuscript repositories.

Kinds of Archival and Manuscript Libraries

One of the most important types of manuscript repository is the official archive which preserves the records of federal, state, or local governmental bodies. Heading this list is the National Archives in Washington, a vast enterprise housing and making available for use the records of all units of the federal government from Revolutionary days to the present, and including materials on the executive, the Congress, the federal courts, and the military establishments.

Similarly the various state archives, though more modest in size and scope, collect and preserve the records of the multitudinous operations of territorial and state governments and often of county, township, or similar subdivisions of the commonwealths. Some of these state archival agencies collect official archival records exclusively or nearly exclusively. Others also collect personal papers and miscellaneous historical material. In many cases these archival agencies form divisions of state historical societies or state libraries. Whether or not they perform the archival function for the state, a number of state historical societies (Wisconsin and Minnesota for example) have developed impressive manuscript collections. (For a comprehensive survey of the archival programs in all fifty states see Ernst Posner, _American State Archives_, Chicago, 1964).

Sometimes libraries include the museum and manuscript functions. The presidential libraries all have extensive museums which help support their manuscript divisions. Occasionally the manuscript library is under the direction of the museum as was the case at Michigan State University for several years. Since manuscripts and artifacts are often located together there is some logic to this arrangement, but because the aim of the museum is to serve the general public while a manuscript library serves principally the much smaller scholarly community, there is a danger that the museum may overshadow the library and limit growth.

Conflict of interest can also appear when a manuscript collection or division is part of a large general library system. There is a danger that book-cataloging methods may be imposed on manuscripts or that book circulation standards may be applied to the use of manuscripts or in determining budget allocations. Those responsible for the operation of the manuscript section of the library must clearly recognize the fundamental differences in treatment and use between books and manuscripts and successfully interpret this difference to higher administrative levels. Many large public libraries such as those of New York and Detroit maintain important manuscript sections and of course America's most distinguished library, the Library of Congress, also houses one of the nation's greatest manuscript collections. Many university libraries contain significant manuscript divisions, for example the library of Duke University and the regional collection in the Cornell Library. Strong programs generally result when manuscript divisions are given a large degree of autonomy in allowing them to pursue their own policies in matters of acquisitions, arrangement, and use.

Finally there are the manuscript libraries founded and managed as independent or virtually independent units devoted primarily to acquisition, preservation, and preparation of manuscripts and rare books. In some cases these libraries were established to house large private holdings of wealthy collectors, among them Huntington in San Marino and Clements in Ann Arbor; in others they house the manuscript treasures assembled by private historical societies, such as those of Pennsylvania and Massachusetts.

The types of libraries mentioned thus far are all effective institutions for preserving mankind's written records. There are, however, many manuscript collections scattered throughout the country which fail to meet even the most modest requirements for effective service. The two worst offenders are local historical societies and small public libraries. Many communities have a group of citizens who, having more than a passing interest in the history of the town or area, form a local historical society. By 1962 there were over 1750 historical societies in the U.S. (Clifford L. Lord, Reuben Gold Thwaites and the Progressive Historical Society Historical Society of Michigan, 1963 p. 5). Sometimes they start a local museum, which properly conducted can serve a useful educational function. However, overzealousness and misconception of function all too frequently lead to dismal results. A handful of Civil War letters are placed in an exhibit case with an assortment of artifacts. Perhaps they are important, perhaps not, but no Civil War historian is ever likely to know. They are as good as lost since there will be no listing of them in the usual guides to manuscript resources. Even if an historian were to discover them, he might well be told that they were only for display. Or the amateur curator of a historical museum may have a few manuscripts of significance, which he allows to be handled by every visitor who comes by with the result that they soon are tattered and torn.

Without a staff trained in manuscript care, local libraries or societies will find manuscripts more of a problem than a blessing. Since they cannot be cataloged by library rules they may go uncataloged or be placed in a virtually unworkable vertical file system or piled in cartons in the basement storage room. The point need not be labored, further. There are proper places for manuscripts and there are improper ones.

Minimum criteria should be met by any library which aspires to collect manuscripts. First, the quarters for housing the manuscripts should be fireproof. To gather manuscripts from many barns and attics into one non-fireproof structure only increases the potential loss by fire.

Second, the collections should be available to researchers at an accessible location and on a regular basis. The widow of a state governor had to be discouraged from having an important collection of her husband's papers left at their original site. To be sure the building was fireproof, but it was located at the governor's summer home on a remote island virtually inaccessible for eight months of the year. In another instance a public library in a medium-sized Midwestern city kept its manuscripts in a locked room. Only for brief periods and on rare occasions was it available for use. Maintaining a regular schedule of hours, preferably daily, is not an unreasonable requirement. In collections available "by appointment only" or on the basis of infrequent and irregular hours the material is virtually inaccessible to scholars.

Third, if the manuscript collection is to be usable it must have professional care. The person responsible for the collection should know how to do research himself so that he can appreciate the problems of visiting scholars. He should know the broad historical background around which his manuscripts center so that he can properly evaluate them. Also, he must know the special techniques of caring for and cataloging manuscripts. To find such a person may not be easy. For the organization with a small budget it may seem impossible. Yet in all fairness to history and the documents these requirements should be met and if they cannot be met, the idea of maintaining a manuscript library should be abandoned, for there are numerous libraries willing and able to provide professional service. Recently a public library in Michigan having no trained archivist and seeing no immediate prospect of getting one, squarely faced the issue and deposited its valuable manuscript collection with a university offering professional care, the only justifiable solution for a library with no professionally equipped manuscript librarian. In this case the materials were placed on deposit with the provision that the community may retrieve them if at some future date it can afford adequate quarters and a professional archivist.

Another solution is for two, three, or more small institutions to pool their funds and hire a trained archivist who can guide their activities and catalog their holdings. This solution is practical for the small college whose budget does not justify a full-time archivist, but which is financially able to share the expense and benefits with two or three neighboring institutions. Such a project is in the planning stage for two Midwestern liberal arts colleges and a regional museum with manuscript collections.

If the library is to have regular hours, adequate buildings, and a professional curator, it must have a permanent financial base. This usually means a measure of local or state support or institutional financing supplied by a business firm, a college, or a foundation. To count on annual voluntary contributions or the support of a single wealthy individual is to court disaster; it may be adequate for a time, but may at any time leave the organization without support. For example, a local historical museum and manuscript library enjoyed the generous support of a wealthy patron during her lifetime, but on her death was forced to curtail its activities drastically and its future now is in doubt because continuing support is inadequate.

Charging fees for use of the collections is never a desirable basis for support. Revenue will be inadequate and research will be hindered. One small Pennsylvania depository has the novel system of charging only when the researcher finds something of use to him. Such a tenuous economic base is woefully inadequate.

Such are the minimum standards for a manuscript library. They fall far short of the optimum. Ideally there should be fireproof quarters, adequate to fulfill existing stack, office, and public service functions of the library and to meet future needs. Enough archives and manuscript libraries have been constructed in the U. S. so that new quarters which meet their special requirements (fumigating, cleaning, sorting rooms, researchers' carrels, exhibit and public rooms) can be designed and built with confidence.

Staff should expand as the library grows, allowing for specialization of staff, with persons to handle readers' services, field work and processing. All of this takes money. Though large financial resources will not guarantee a first-rate program, all first-rate manuscript libraries have operating budgets that permit competitive salaries for at least two or three professionals.

Objectives of the Manuscript Library

Whether it be a one-man operation or a well-endowed organization with a large staff, a well thought out, carefully drawn objective or objectives for its manuscript collection is of fundamental importance to the library. Unfortunately many manuscript libraries collect manuscripts *per se* regardless of whether they have any relationship to each other or even whether they have any research value. Educational institutions, encouraged by professional historians seeking resources for their graduate students, have offended in this way. Even small undergraduate colleges which require honors papers from seniors feel they should gather a few boxes of odds and ends of manuscripts for the students to use. In so doing they overlook a vast quantity of primary source material of considerably greater research value to their students, for example a microfilm file of the New York *Times* or other newspapers, state and federal documents, or the rich body of published manuscripts or manuscripts available at reasonable cost on microfilm from the federal archives or other depositories. It is better for a small college library to acquire the superbly edited eight volumes of his correspondence than to hold four or five holograph Theodore Roosevelt letters. Unplanned, indiscriminate collecting of manuscripts by any institution is not in the best interest of scholarship in general or the historical profession in particular. The primary purpose of a manuscript collection should be to serve the world of scholarship. This does not mean that amateur researchers, school children, or local lay interests can be ignored in planning a collection. These groups would be the principal users of a museum, but they will form a very small percentage of the manuscript library's patrons (see Chapter IX). The manuscript library, by its very nature, is aimed primarily at the scholar rather than at the general reader and this fact should determine its collecting policies.

Other factors to be considered in choosing the collection's theme are its geographical location and its proximity to other manuscript libraries, the institution supporting it, the financial resources behind it, the space and staff it has or can expect to have, and lastly the fundamental one of how the collection can best serve scholarship. With these considerations in mind, the aim(s) or theme(s) can be chosen.

One of the most common and most successful themes is a geographical one. The theme of most state historical societies' libraries such as Minnesota, Ohio, Iowa, is their state. In like manner, a state-wide institutional manuscript library like the Michigan Historical Collections of the University of Michigan uses the state as its collecting theme. Or the theme may be a portion of a state like the Cornell University regional collection. There are endless numbers of geographical subdivisions that can be used. The geographical theme is logical, workable, and generally satisfactory provided that the geographical area chosen is not too large for the library to cover adequately or that it does not overlap and compete with established libraries.

This question of overlapping and competition is a serious problem and it is getting worse. Inevitably, there will be some overlapping and some competition among the collecting policies of various repositories. A library with state-wide interests will overlap with a depository gathering materials dealing with a city in that state, but this need not be serious unless either institutions switches its primary collecting interests to the same area as the other. Some competition is probably helpful in keeping a library alert. On the other hand establishing a collection with a theme almost identical to that of another library can lead to hard feelings, wasteful duplication of effort, a diffusion of manuscripts which should be in one place or even the splitting of collections. In one state, for example, the correspondence of a Civil War general ended up in one depository's files, his diaries in another. Such practices reflect little credit on the institutions involved or on the profession itself.

Such duplication is made even more absurd by the fact that there are limitless possibilities for selecting objectives which do not conflict, which will serve the scholarly public and which can bring credit to the parent institution. For example, a developing university manuscript library with limited funds for purchasing but with imaginative leadership saw that no one in its region was collecting materials on twentieth century industrial unionism. The university is centered in a major industrial city long important for its role in the labor movement. Its program was carefully worked out, staff expanded to meet the influx of materials, and substantial financial assistance eventually obtained from the union itself. In seven years it has come far on the road to becoming a major research center for recent labor history.

Collecting can be focused on almost anything that has a history which can be derived from written records. Business, literature, agriculture, medicine are all proper themes. Or a library can be organized around a significant personality, as are the presidential libraries. Centered around the presidential papers, these manuscript libraries have assembled important related collections, such as the papers of cabinet members, associates, or congressional contemporaries. Such manuscript depositories, by their very nature, also have a time period theme roughly equivalent to the president's life span. Some libraries, in fact, make use of the time period exclusively as their theme. If rigidly adhered to such a theme, limited by time, will mean the fossilization of the library as its collecting diminishes. This fossilizing is not necessarily bad, but it will bring a shift in its program and attract a different type of staff. The emphasis will turn to perfecting the processing of its materials and perhaps to edited publication of its holdings. A geographical or subject theme will avoid this fossilization although interest in the library's holdings may wax and wane as time and historical interests change.

The point should be clear enough; with but a little imagination and a keen appraisal of the manuscript library's setting, backing, and potential growth, a theme can be selected which will give meaning to the library, avoid duplication of effort, allow for expansion, and contribute positively to scholarly research.

Types of Manuscript to be Collected

Manuscripts take several forms, some more useful than others. A field representative returning to the library with the papers of a prominent citizen is likely to be asked by a colleague,

"How much correspondence did you get?" This is a valid query and one which reflects the importance the experienced collector attaches to this type of manuscript. Personal correspondence, hopefully both letters received and copies of letters sent, is usually the most significant type of manuscript material, especially if the files are complete. Organizational and institutional correspondence can be revealing too, but there is much more likelihood of finding routine material, which is frequently repetitious and consequently of little or no research value.

Individuals may also have saved diaries, personal account books, scrapbooks, notebooks, manuscript speeches and articles. For institutions, organizations, and businesses there may be minutes, reports, ledgers, journals, and all kinds of financial records.

Not all have the same importance. Quality varies widely and just because something is in manuscript form and therefore presumably unique, it need not automatically be kept. If space is a problem, and there are few libraries where it is not, a decision has to be made about which manuscripts to keep and which to reject.* Even if space were not a problem, the question of the historical value of the material is pertinent, and should be raised by every collecting agency about every accession. For example, a business firm with origins in the first half of the nineteenth century may offer you its records. You find upon examination that they consist of hundreds of volumes of ledgers, account books, journals, stockholders lists, cancelled checks, and other financial records. The correspondence files and minutes of the company have been lost or are not available for deposit. The question then arises, should the collecting agency accept such a body of records where all the policy making documents are no longer in existence? Though individual circumstances make impossible a general rule, the answer probably should be no.

This example raises the fundamental question of who should determine the research value of a collection. Basically it must rest with the library staff--an added reason, if any were needed, to

*This problem of selectivity is discussed in detail in Chapter V.

insist on an able staff and as large a one as possible. But there are also avenues for getting outside help either formally or informally. The library may set up a small committee of professional historians or other competent scholars to solve this problem. (Harvard University uses this system in handling its archival material.) Informal advice can be obtained from professional historians in nearby colleges or universities, state archives, or historical libraries.

Research value is not, nor should it be, the only criterion in accepting or judging a manuscript collection, although it must be the primary consideration if the library presumes to serve the needs of scholars. There are also the interests of antiquarians and manuscript enthusiasts to be considered. For the general public and the non-research oriented person the rare, antiquarian, manuscript may have more interest and appeal than research materials. For example, the original of a significant Indian treaty whose content may be fully known may excite greater popular interest when displayed in a library's showcase than the minutes of a Negro improvement society of the 1930's, even though the latter may have considerable research potential and the former, none. A depository in a midwestern state recently received a small collection of its first governor's papers. This included a manuscript of his inaugural address and a small collection of letters of prominent citizens in the state and nation. Since most of the information in these items was already known, their research value was slight, but public interest aroused by the gift was very valuable to the library. Such collections can add considerable prestige to an institution. They make fine exhibit items, they endear you to patriotic societies (the gubernatorial collection described above was laminated by funds eagerly supplied by such a group) and, to be honest, even the most dedicated scholar gets at least a little thrill from handling an original Lincoln letter, even though a complete and accurate copy may be available in print.

The library will also have to consider other materials not strictly manuscript in form. One basic question is whether or not the library should collect printed materials to supplement is manuscript holdings. Every manuscript library should either own or have convenient access to a shelf of standard biographical and general reference works. These books are essential for cataloging purposes and are useful for researchers. But how far should the library go beyond this point? True, a printed collection arranged around the same theme or themes as the manuscript holdings is a valuable asset to the staff and to researchers. It is also true that printed materials frequently accompany the manuscripts. The determining factors in settling this question are usually: space, availability of printed materials nearby, and the interests of the library.

The experience of the Michigan Historical Collections of the University of Michigan may offer some guidance in this regard. These collections of materials of state-wide interests are located at a university with extensive library holdings. Standard reference works (which are duplicated in the University library), the published works of persons whose papers it has (these may or may not duplicate other holdings), and most important, printed materials about Michigan not found in other campus libraries, including local histories, published reminiscences, proceedings of religious denominations, trade publications, house organs and similar material are acquired selectively. The experience of this library and many others has been that such a printed collection is of great value.

Broadsides and handbills too are useful for information or for display. These items as well as leaflets and booklets do pose a storage and organization problem, but a good vertical file system which permits small items to be filed upright and larger items to be shelved flat is an effective solution.

Printed materials such as clippings or pamphlets will frequently form an integral part of the manuscript collection they accompany. If so they should be kept with the collection rather than dispersed. Such materials reflect the person who collected them and any tampering with them (except for the removal of unannotated duplicates) would reduce the value and usefulness of the collection.

Newspapers will prove a particularly useful adjunct to a manuscript collection. Though often presenting a one dimensional, slanted view of events, they frequently are the only source available on a wide variety of subjects. Much of the history of the Populist Movement in the U.S. has been written from newspaper sources because manuscript sources are so meager. But newspapers pose serious problems too, the greatest of which is bulk. A long file of a daily paper can require an enormous amount of space, and the problem of physical deterioration must be met. When newspapers shifted late in the nineteenth century from rag to pulp paper, preservation in their original form became nearly impossible. There are solutions, all of which require money. Microfilm is one. It reduces bulk to a manageable size and is more permanent than pulp newsprint, but it is expensive and is more difficult to use.

Perhaps a compromise solution is for the library to make a selective sampling of newspapers in its collecting area, permanently preserving those files printed on rag paper, microfilming those volumes on pulp paper. In selecting the representative papers for a geographical area, the newspaper's political affiliation, its rural or urban nature and its coverage all are factors to be taken into account. Special cause newspapers are especially valuable since they represent a special constituency or point of view. These are frequently of considerable significance to historians and often are most difficult to find because many of them have relatively short runs. For example, to date not a single issue can be located of a newspaper published in the 1840's by a southwestern Michigan communitarian association, even though membership lists are extant and a thorough search has been made.

Newspapers are an essential complement to the holdings of some collections. A fine labor archives, though collecting important personal papers of labor leaders and correspondence files, minutes, and other manuscripts of the union locals, also has assembled a large assortment of small local newspapers, some published only in mimeographed form. Whether essential or not, a supplementary newspaper collection is a helpful and significant adjunct to most manuscript libraries.

Sooner or later every manuscript library will be offered

pictures and must decide whether to accept them. It has three alternatives: it can refuse them, it can make pictures a major interest in its collecting, or it can accept and care for those pictures which accompany other gifts. Usually the third alternative is chosen. Photographs are useful display items, and since they are in demand by all news media, they have public relations value.

The newest method of collecting historical data, developed extensively in recent years by institutions like Columbia University and the Ford Archives, is the oral history interview. If done correctly and professionally, oral interviews can be most useful to the historian, particularly in adding flesh and blood, color and details to a study whose basic facts are established from other sources. On the other hand the material, if not properly collected, can be worthless.

Before undertaking an oral history program the manuscript library should examine the results achieved by experienced collectors in this field, and consider whether the program is worth the substantial commitment it entails. Oral history is the most expensive form of collecting, other than the acquisition of manuscripts by direct purchase, because it requires such a heavy allotment of staff time. A skilled interviewer is essential in carrying out a successful program. He must have personal characteristics that will inspire confidence in the persons he will meet, put them at ease, and draw from them the desired information without injecting his own views and personal feelings. He should know the history, and must be an expert in the specific subject area of the interviewee's contribution. An interviewer seeking oral data concerning life in a Colorado silver mining town should be thoroughly familiar with the history of the town in general, the chronology of important events in the region, and the leaders in the area.

Such detailed and extensive knowledge makes it imperative to conduct a number of interviews with different persons on the same subject. Thus almost any significant oral history project will require a carefully conceived and comprehensive approach to the subject and will not be a single shot affair.

An example of a good oral history project is one conducted

by The University of Michigan-Wayne State University Institute of Industrial Relations on industrial labor unionism in the twentieth century. A faculty member, well versed in labor history, with ample secretarial assistance was given the assignment of locating workers and union leaders significant in the UAW and in the founding of the CIO. The interviewer, thoroughly familiar with the subject area himself, had preliminary non-recorded talks with his contacts to establish rapport and to outline the nature of the proposed interview. Then followed the tape recording sessions which varied in length and frequently involved several meetings. The tapes were transcribed, a copy returned to the speaker, corrected by him, and then retyped in triplicate for permanent preservation. The interviews were signed and dated, and copies were given to the person interviewed, to the Wayne State University Labor History Archives and to the Michigan Historical Collections of The University of Michigan. As of January 1, 1964, 155 persons had been interviewed over a six year period at a cost of $46,000. The result is a superb collection of materials on one facet of the American labor movement.

Summary

The number of archival and manuscript libraries is growing. These institutions take many forms--governmental archives, historical society collections, museum-manuscript libraries, general libraries with a manuscript section and others. For the most part they perform their functions competently, but there are other groups engaging in collecting manuscript materials who are not suited for the task. Particularly ill equipped are small local historical societies or small libraries lacking adequate quarters and professional staff. All agencies undertaking the collection of manuscripts should meet minimum standards.

A new manuscript library should have a theme or themes around which its collecting program is organized, giving it meaning and character and avoiding duplication of established libraries. The possibilities for themes are limitless, but they should be based on the library's own character, location and potential.

After deciding upon a theme the library will have to consider the various types of manuscripts available and their possible use. In like manner they will have to consider whether or not to collect supplementary printed material, photographic records and oral histories. If the decision is to collect any or all of these, the library will have to recognize and make provision for the special requirements each poses.

Suggested Readings

Historical Societies:

C. M. Silvestro and R. O. Williams, A Look at Ourselves. Madison 1962.

Walter Muir Whitehill, Independent Historical Societies: An Enquiry into Their Research and Publication Functions. Cambridge, 1964.

Robert L. Brubaker, "Manuscript Collections," Library Trends, XIII (October, 1964), pp. 226-253.

Collecting Policies:

Lewis G. Vander Velde,"Local Records," The American Archivist, III (October, 1940), pp. 251-260.

Thomas P. Martin, "A Manuscript Collecting Venture in the Middle West: Indiana, 1950-1953," The American Archivist, XVII (October, 1954), pp. 305-312.

Lucile Kane, "Collecting Policies of the Minnesota Historical Society, 1849-1952," The American Archivist, XVI (April, 1953), pp. 127-136.

David C. Duniway, "Conflicts in Collecting," The American Archivist, XXIV (January, 1961), pp. 55-63.

Oral History:

Saul Benison, "Reflections on Oral History," The American Archivist, XXVIII (January, 1965), pp. 71-77.

Gould P. Colman, "Oral History--An Appeal for More Systematic Procedures," The American Archivist, XXVIII (January, 1965), pp. 79-83.

Charles T. Morrissey, "Truman and the Presidency Records and Oral Reflections," The American Archivist, XXVIII (January, 1965), pp. 53-61.

Donald C. Swain, "Problems for Practitioners of Oral History," The American Archivist, XXVIII (January, 1965), pp. 63-69.

Vaughn Davis Burnett, "Oral History Can be Worthwhile," The American Archivist, XVIII (July, 1955), pp. 241-253.

Owen W. Bombard, "A New Measure of Things Past," The American Archivist, XVIII (April, 1955), pp. 123-132.

Chapter II

How to Collect

Somebody must do some collecting before there can be a manuscript library. As Thomas Le Duc wrote in the American Archivist: "The prime task of the archivist is to gather; he must be a shameless solicitor and a ruthless collector. What today seems trivial may tomorrow be indispensable." ("Arcana Siwash, The Functions and Needs of a College Archives," The American Archivist, IX (April, 1946), p. 135). The growth and development of a library is determined by its collecting program and how and in what areas this collecting is done will shape its character.

Methods of Collecting

The kinds of material sought will determine the method of collecting. Very rare manuscript material, such as the papers of the signers of the Declaration of Independence, Civil War generals, or early presidents of the United States, usually will have to be acquired by purchase. On the other hand, if the library's objective is to build a collection of manuscripts dealing with local history or the history of some institution, desirable materials can be obtained by a well organized solicitation of potential donors.

In acquisition by purchase the most important ingredient for success is money, and the collecting of rare manuscript material or even some items of local significance requires sizeable outlays. William L. Clements, benefactor of the famous library bearing his name, paid more than $300,000 to acquire six important manuscript collections dealing with the American Revolution. In 1944 a single-sentence statement on the Emancipation Proclamation written and signed by Abraham Lincoln sold for $2,500. (Colton Storm and Howard Peckham, Invitation to Book Collecting, Its Pleasures and Practices. New York, 1947, pp. 120, 125).

With money in hand the next step is to ferret out the material. This task is simpler than seeking gifts, for manuscripts for sale are usually advertised. Most rare book and manuscript dealers publish catalogs which are frequently interesting documents in themselves. Though seldom a complete listing of the dealer's stock, the catalog provides a sampling of his wares and indicates the scope of his holdings. When you are fortunate enough to discover a desirable manuscript collection, order it by telephone rather than letter or you may find yourself outmaneuvered by a more enterprising collector. Most dealers will allow you to order on approval. This is good practice for the library then knows what it is getting and the dealer will not have to cope with dissatisfied customers. The library's only obligation is to decide promptly whether to buy the manuscripts or return them.

Over the years, a library should establish personal relationships with dealers throughout the country. Needless to say the more your institution spends with a dealer, the better the relationship. Dealers can be of considerable assistance. They become familiar with the library's holdings, its special wants and needs, and are able to channel materials to your institution before public announcement. Care must be exercised in selecting dealers to make sure they are reliable, honest, and intelligent. Without these qualities a dealer may prove a liability rather than an asset. The rare book and manuscript trade does have its charlatans and deceivers, and cautious dealings are called for.

Frequently manuscripts are offered for sale at auction. Some of these sales are widely publicized among collectors, and the books and papers to be sold are described. At other times estates which include manuscript and printed items are broken up and the manuscripts sold unopened, which increases the risk in buying them. Unless the nature or background of papers is known, it is best to leave them for professional dealers. The occasional good find will not outweigh the mistakes. Although at times real bargains can be obtained, the results of collecting by purchase are almost directly proportionate to the amount of money spent. Purchase money can best be used by seeking manuscripts not closely related to those already deposited in manuscript libraries or in great demand by dealers and collectors. These areas are not easy to find, and the manuscript library supported largely by public funds is at a real disadvantage in collecting by purchase. The depository is in fact in direct competition with literally hundreds of wealthy private autograph and manuscript collectors, and with richly endowed libraries. A few affluent collectors can soon absorb the materials in any area. One businessman, for example, has procured most of the Walt Whitman manuscript materials that are not already in libraries and is in a position to meet any competition for new materials that appear on the market. It would be foolish, therefore, for a library to undertake an active program of collecting Whitman manuscripts. It would be pointless to attempt to acquire comprehensive collections of U.S. Presidents' papers because nearly all of them are in the possession of well established libraries.

A further complication is an inflated market. Prosperity has raised the price of manuscripts along with the general price level. More people are drawn into collecting, for they have money to spend, thus expanding the market and raising prices. Prices, too, are influenced by collecting fads. In the early 1960's, for example, with Civil War publications appearing at the rate of two or three volumes for every engagement, major and minor, Civil War manuscripts and related items commanded unusually high prices. Dealers' catalogs offered undistinguished letters of unknown soldiers for as much as twenty-five or thirty dollars apiece.

The trend toward collecting by purchase is growing. New depositories seeking to acquire significant research materials quickly, perhaps sponsored by a well-to-do friend, are acquiring collections in this manner. They are not buying rare manuscripts of national significance sold by professional dealers but state, local, and regional materials which previously had no market. These are not purchased through dealers but from the family or the firm in which the manuscripts originated. Non-professional sellers of documents usually over-estimate the value of their holdings. If a document is old, they conclude that it is automatically valuable and ask for compensation accordingly.

Collecting manuscripts by solicitation requires diplomatic skill and the patience of Job. That patience (and persistence) is a necessary virtue is well illustrated by the history of one important collection acquired by a state university. From the time the first request for papers was made until the moving van arrived from Washington with two tons of manuscripts, nearly twenty-three years had elapsed.

Choosing a Collecting Theme

To collect successfully there must be a plan, not a spur of the moment inspiration but a carefully-drawn, thoughtful program that implements the main purpose of the library. A logical beginning is to decide on particular themes around which your collecting will center. Selecting these themes is most important, for as noted in Chapter I, their choice will determine the library's character and development. If a political theme is chosen, the political history of a city for example, a good starting place would be to find the names of all the mayors, discover the place of residence of those still living and the whereabouts of the relatives or descendents of those deceased. This first step is no easy task, even though the history of the community may not extend beyond three quarters of a century. The mayors' names can be easily found, but tracing descendents can lead into complex genealogical research and incidentally to interesting collecting enterprises not conceived in the original plan. In addition to the mayoralty records the library can logically seek the papers of defeated candidates. Although they may not have been famous, their papers and those of other less known figures often contain more material for the scholar than those of a "big name" politician whose surviving papers may consist of only a bound volume of testimonial letters, a few diplomas and assorted mementoes.

The papers of city councilmen, political party leaders, nationality and political clubs, and other persons and organizations also can be acquired, adding depth to the library's holdings. The Presidential libraries not only collect the papers of the president and his family but also of persons connected with his administration, his pre-presidential years, and sometimes, also, the papers of other contemporaries, such as senators and congressmen, whose papers throw light on the period.

This same general approach can be used to gather materials of a prominent individual when none of his papers exist or where those that do exist do not present a full portrait. This approach has been used in connection with Senator Arthur H. Vandenberg, active in Michigan politics from the first years of the twentieth century. Although an important body of his personal papers was available, it left many gaps. To attempt to fill out the picture, an extensive campaign of contacting persons known or surmised to be his correspondents, particularly in his home town of Grand Rapids was undertaken. This program, though it ran into many dead ends and fell short of providing a complete research collection, did turn up much significant Vandenberg material, including letters to his physician, a superb scrapbook collection, and extensive correspondence dating back to 1910.

The theme or subject approach is useful not only for collecting the papers of individuals but also of institutions and organizations. Perhaps the library wishes to collect the papers of agricultural organizations. It could well begin with the Grange, still an active organization whose state headquarters can provide records of annual meetings, minutes of its executive committee (or tell you where they are preserved) and supply you with a roster of local affiliates and past leaders who are likely donors. Eventually, the record accumulated can give a comprehensive picture of all levels of the organization's activities and policies, and leads may be obtained concerning antecedent, competitive and affiliate groups which can then be pursued.

The records of colleges, universities, religious denominations, professional societies, and similar groups lend themselves to this type of collecting. But the library may ask, quite naturally, will we not be overwhelmed if we use this approach systematically and diligently? If we collect all the city councilmen's papers or all the records of every local grange, where can they be put and will we be serving history to save them all?

This problem is not so formidable as it might seem at first glance. Natural attrition brings a partial solution. Through the years papers will have been lost, destroyed by fire, or will have met with similar misfortunes. Despite these contingencies the fact remains that large bodies of papers may have been saved, posing the problem of what to accept and what to reject. In beginning a collection the tendency is to accept virtually everything. Empty shelf space abounds, and there is a strong desire to please everyone and to build good will for the library. As the library matures, shelves fill up and selectivity becomes essential. Selection should really be practiced from the beginning and every effort should be made to keep acquisitions pertinent and high in quality. Nothing is gained by filling shelves with papers having no research potential or no relation to the area or subject around which the library is building its holdings.

Following Leads

Following leads which provide information concerning the whereabouts of known or possible collections of manuscripts is another effective aid to collecting. Frequently these leads come from previous donors. As the roster of donors grows, it will include a few very interested individuals who will suggest others who may have materials. The local history enthusiast will attract people from throughout his region who come to show him historical materials or give information. Such friends of the library scattered throughout the area of coverage, are more aware of local conditions and developments than the library staff. Friends connected with an institution or organization about which you are seeking materials can also be of value. An exceptionally extensive and high quality manuscript collection of one of the religious denominations was assembled because a well-known clergyman within the denomination made it his hobby during his retirement years to collect these records for deposit in a regional library.

Of course some of these friends may become problems. They may want the library to collect inappropriate items. They may misrepresent you to possible donors. They may prove to be your friend merely to acquire special privileges and favors. Perhaps their most common fault is simply taking too much staff time. But despite these potential drawbacks their overall record is one of helpfulness and valuable assistance.

Occasionally a library will find it advantageous to organize persons interested in its work into formal associations, especially if large sums of money are needed for purchase of rare items. Though these groups are usually oriented towards financial support of the library, they may also serve to stimulate manuscript collecting. (See Chapter IX).

Donors are frequently willing to assist by arranging appointments with other persons in the community whom you wish to approach--always an advantage when starting with no previous contact, and many of them are willing to do a little address hunting, find certain family relationships, and perform similar services. If the library is connected with an institution of higher education, alumni, faculty, and staff members are a rich source of leads. Naturally sympathetic to your endeavors, they can be useful as sources of material (especially so in collecting manuscripts for a university archives) and as suppliers of information on possible sources.

Occasionally the scholar who uses your materials uncovers other manuscripts or makes valuable suggestions based on his special knowledge of the subject. He will prove your most valuable helper because he knows the importance of the material he has used or would like to use, and his familiarity with his subject suggests sources to him that might be overlooked by someone less knowledgeable.

Reaching the Potential Donor

To locate the whereabouts of desired manuscripts is one thing; to procure them is another. First of all the library must reach the potential donor. A letter written under the institution's letterhead, containing information about the library, its origins, location, and objectives, is the best first step. Examples of materials in the library, carefully chosen to illustrate its scope and the connection between existing holdings and the proposed new collection should be described. The letter should also specify the type of papers desired, i.e., correspondence files, diaries, scrapbooks.

Description of the kinds of papers you want is important, for many persons contacted about "papers" interpret the term very narrowly to mean citations, diplomas, published works, rather than the historically more important informal materials such as letter files. It is good policy to invite the prospective donor to visit your collection (and mean it!), and if possible suggest that someone from the library will call for further discussion of the matter.

The next step is to await a reply, which may be promptly forthcoming or may not come at all. Silence is no reason for discouragement. Every experienced collector knows that few initial letters bring immediate response. After a reasonable interval, and you must use your own judgment as to how long this is, write again or telephone. The important thing is to reach the prospective donor. If you fail to get an answer to your inquiries, pay a visit anyway. More often than not you will be greeted by "Oh, I have been intending to write!" The need for personal contact with the prospective donor cannot be overemphasized. Whether it is done at the library or out in the field is not so important as the fact that it takes place. The donor will be flattered. He now knows the institution is serious about its request and he can personally assess the nature of the library and its interests. The library in turn can make a much fuller and stronger presentation of its case by personal visit and can, at the same time, assay the value of the materials. Even if the donor defers relinquishing the papers, the personal call has opened the door.

Since the personal visit is so important, the person or persons selected to perform this service must be chosen with great care. Funds invested in the support of a good field man will bring in more in terms of the value of collections than will the same amount used for purchasing materials.

What should be the qualifications of the prospective field representative? He should be a mature and attractive person who can suitably represent the sponsoring institution. He should like people and should be at ease in the millionaire's club or the farmer's barn. Conversation should come naturally and pleasantly with no affectation. He should be interested in history and should know the importance of the historical manuscripts he finds. He must be persistent and patient enough to search out and acquire a collection even though the task may be a long one. It should go without saying that he must be a person of integrity and sincerity, for an insincere person who tries to pretend will surely disappoint himself and his institution.

Besides the letter and visit there are other ways to seek out materials, though none is so effective as the personal touch. Radio and television are obvious channels. Through them you can reach a large audience, making contact with far more persons than by personal letter. These appeals for historical manuscripts or information can uncover some desirable items, but general solicitations are usually disappointing. An offer of money will result in a wider response; otherwise few will answer and those who do will offer commonplace items, land patents, family Bibles, or an ordinary published historical volume. It may be worth trying, but do not expect great results. Handbills are even less effective. Some years ago a manuscript library drew up and had printed an attractive one page broadside identifying the library and its purpose and asking for materials. Literally thousands of these were distributed. To this day not one document in the library can be directly attributed to this solicitation.

A more personal (and thus more effective) method of solicitation than radio, T.V., newspaper, or handbills is speech-making by staff members. Though the subject may not be the library itself, members of the audience will often ask about the program of the library or better still volunteer materials they possess. A group that has never heard a discussion of the needs of preserving and depositing historical manuscripts will be much more responsive than a local historical society that already has been solicited a dozen times.

General Conditions Affecting the Collecting Program

Numerous imprecise and intangible factors affect solicitation efforts. The timing of the appeal, its form and content and the effectiveness of the field representative's planning and personal contacts, all will influence the ultimate results. No rigid rules can cover these factors. They will be properly handled if high quality personnel conducts the operation. The quality of the staff, for that matter, will determine in large measure the prestige and stature of the library. Imposing quarters are also a major asset, but even their absence can in part be compensated for by a clean, attractive and well-ordered physical plant with neatly shelved materials. The appearance of a library can be the determining factor in a donor's choice of a repository

Transporting the Collection

After locating and receiving a collection, there remains the logistic problem of getting the collection to the library. If contacts have all been by mail and the collection is not bulky, for example, a set of diaries or a few letter files, the safest and easiest method is to have them sent by mail or by express; preferably the latter because the express company will pick up and deliver and material can be sent collect The library should always offer to pay the shipping costs, whatever form they may take.

If a collection is very large, it is wise to send someone to examine it. Especially if there has been no personal contact before, this trip can serve to weed out items of no value to the library. At this stage it is usually better to take too much, discarding later, than to risk abandoning materials of consequence. It is also wise, though sometimes circumstances do not permit, for this preliminary sorting to be accomplished with no assistance or advice from the donor. Reviewing the material may make the prospective donor sentimental and nostalgic, leading to endless recounting of family anecdotes or even worse, to second thoughts about parting with the items. The donor may wish you to take materials that you do not want. There can be no rules to cover such situations. Generally if the reason for not taking certain material is presented clearly the donor will understand why some items are not pertinent to a collection and will not insist on their inclusion. On the other hand, there are times when something has to be taken for the sake of diplomary rather than history.

The library, in any case, should be careful about accepting quantities of material which it is obligated to keep regardless of value. A solution that is frequently agreeable to all is for the library to promise to return to the donor materials it does not wish to retain. Not unfrequently the field agent finds himself actively engaged in personally hunting out the materials he is to examine. This may mean opening trunks, poking around musty basements, crawling under the rafters of dust-encrusted attics, and exploring little-used barns. On one such adventure documents spanning a hundred years of a family history were found in nearly every room in a large old frame house. Some of the rooms had not been used for fifty years and were accordingly covered with layers of dirt so heavy that even a dust mask failed to prevent a bad case of bronchitis. The search uncovered many important manuscripts, plus some $415 in cash which had been hidden away, in bills of small denomination, in every conceivable place. The library kept the documents, and the heirs were grateful for the money. This search is in contrast to another exploring venture during which the donor rented a suite of hotel rooms for two days and had the several thousand pounds of accumulated records placed there for preliminary sorting in most pleasant surroundings.

Accessioning

Once the material reaches the library it must be accessioned. This is a vital step which, if not accomplished almost at once, is easily overlooked. The accessioning process should be simple. If there are many collections coming in, or if there is delay in processing, or if several staff members may be involved in receiving material, the use of an accession slip is very helpful. This form (see appendix for example) should contain the donor's name and address, the name of any intermediate person handling the papers (a lawyer or friend of the family), the staff member who received the collection, and a one or two sentence description noting size, approximate inclusive dates, and type of papers included. The completed form should be passed on by the accessioner to the manuscript cataloger or attached to the material if it is to be temporarily stored before processing. The main purpose of accessioning is to connect the collection with its donor in the depository's records.

A workable system is this: Beginning with the first donor to the library assign that donor a number, record his number, name, and a brief description of his gift in a book of accessions. Example: No. 163 Mrs. John J. Jones (Mary Smith Jones), Lake City, Colorado. 4 feet of correspondence files, diaries and other family papers of the Albert Smith family ca. 1889-1920. Periodically (weekly or monthly) the donor book information should be transferred to a permanent card file, alphabetically arranged, which should include full mailing address and a more precise listing of materials. If the library places donors on a mailing list, it should be done at this time.

The donor number becomes a very important part of the library's record system. Hereafter all correspondence with Mrs. Jones will be filed by her donor number. This number will appear on the catalog cards covering the Smith collection. If there are not too many documents and bound manuscript items, the donor number can be placed in pencil on the document itself. All subsequent gifts by Mrs. Jones will be listed on her donor card along with the date of their acquisition and the number will continue to be used to indicate her gifts. In fact, it can be used to record gifts from her estate.

Publicity

After accessioning has been completed, the collection is ready for processing and cataloging, but its arrival in the library also calls for other attention. If it is a collection of some importance, it should be publicized. Sometimes a donor will specifically ask for a public announcement, and occasionally may arrange for the publicity himself. If the depository makes the announcement, the news release should, of course, be cleared with the donor.

The publicity can take two forms: articles in public news media and notices in scholarly journals. Each serves a different purpose. News releases to the local paper or, if of broader interest, to the state and national press, serves to publicize the library' program and make known its collecting interests. If the materials are of good quality, unusual, financially valuable, or have human interest potential, it is easy to get this publicity. The other type of publicity in the scholarly journal serves to alert the world of scholarship and potential users of the material to the collection's location and its accessibility for use. If the collection has some national significance, the American Historical Review may give it a brief notice, although this periodical devotes most of its space to accessions of the Library of Congress, National Archives, presidential libraries, and similar nationally-oriented depositories. Both The American Archivist and the Journal of American History are generous in including notices of new accessions in local, state, and regional depositories. The journals of the state historical societies often carry news of recent accessions. The library can publicize its accessions in its own annual report.

There is one other type of publicity that deserves mention, though it should seldom be used. This is the public presentation of a collection at a program sponsored by the library. This usually means printed invitations, speeches, and refreshments. This treatment must be reserved for very special collections, but it can be effective, pleasing the donor and entertaining guests whom you wish to interest.

Expressions of Thanks

Every collection no matter how small deserves a prompt thank you. This expression usually takes the form of a sincere letter of appreciation from the person on the staff with whom the donor had the most contact. An oral thank you should never be allowed to take the place of this more formal expression. If the collection is particularly important, there should be a second letter from the head of the library or sponsoring organization such as the president of the university in the case of a library attached to such an institution. This expression of gratitude may be carried further with a formal resolution from the governing body of the institution, the board of regents of a university or the board of management of a library. The library's annual report, if it contains the names of the donors, serves as an additional formal thank you.

Summary

Collecting can be done by purchase or by solicitation from potential donors. The first requires ample funds and attention to the market; the second, imaginative planning, careful contact arrangements, effective staff work, flexibility and persistence. In soliciting manuscripts a planned approach to donors will greatly facilitate effective collecting. Other useful leads will come from the library's friends. How the approach is made and the effectiveness of the personal contact will determine much of the success of the entire collecting program.

Once the commitment of materials has been secured, transportation must be arranged. If a large collection, it should be surveyed personally by a staff member who may do some rough sorting on the scene. Once at the library, the manuscripts must be accessioned in a simple way that will assure the proper crediting of the gift to the donor. Lastly the collecting agency must unfailingly express its thanks for all materials received.

Suggested Readings

Thomas LeDuc, "Arcana Siwash, The Functions and Needs of a College Archives," The American Archivist, IX (April 1946), pp. 132-35.

Lewis E. Atherton, "Western Historical Manuscript Collection--a Case Study of a Collecting Program," The American Archivist, XXVI (January, 1963), pp. 41-49.

Colton Storm and Howard Peckham, Invitation to Book Collecting, Its Pleasures and Practices. New York, 1947 .

Robert M. Warner, "The Role of the Secular Institution in Collecting Church Records," The American Archivist, XXVIII (April, 1965), pp. 247-254.

Chapter III
Processing a Collection

By processing in this chapter we mean what happens to a manuscript collection from the time it is accessioned until it is ready for cataloging and the preparation of finding aids. Processing can of course be helped or hindered by the collecting and accessioning procedures themselves. If papers are carefully boxed when received from the donor, and if information about the history of the papers and the persons with whom they deal is noted by the recipient, later processing steps can be facilitated.

However, papers will not always be sought or collected by the library. Frequently they will just arrive. They will arrive in soup cartons, ancient suitcases, and brown paper packages as well as in filing boxes. Sometimes they will be clean. More frequently they will carry the accumulated dirt of twenty years of storage in a coal bin or rat infested barn. Occasionally it will have been possible to bring the standard containers used by the manuscript library to the place where the papers have been stored and box them in some semblance of order before they are loaded into car or truck. Usually there will have been no preliminary sorting or cleaning, no attempt to preserve original order. Or even worse they will come in installments as some family member inspects the contents. When this happens every effort should be made to obtain the entire collection before beginning to process it.

Steps Preliminary to Processing

Fortunate indeed is the library with mechanical cleaning devices such as vacuum chambers which fumigate and clean with practically no hand labor. More frequently the manuscript curator must clean by hand; having the dirt accumulate under his nails, soil his clothing, and clog his respiratory tract. Perhaps by way of compensation, one should be reminded that the kind and amount of dirt tells any good manuscript person something about the history of the papers and the family in whose custody they have been. Cleaning and unpacking should be done by a trained person. The experienced manuscript librarian will be able to note any surviving order or sort into rough categories that will make later handling easier. This is not a chore for page or janitor, despite its unpleasant aspects.

At this time documents needing repair or restoration will be removed. There is a temptation to perform minor repairs in the library itself. If it is fortunate enough to have a staff member who is trained to do mending and binding this will be very satisfactory. Most libraries do not. This is not work for amateurs, particularly when the materials to be worked on have great intrinsic value. Clippings can safely be mounted and minor tears repaired by using tissue and flour and water paste. More complicated jobs should be sent to an expert.

In the course of unpacking and cleaning the cataloging units will fall into place almost automatically. Is this collection the papers of a family, multi-generational in scope, but nonetheless inherently a single unit? Is it really two collections, the papers of an individual or a family but also the records of a business firm only peripherally related to the family, more properly forming two units for cataloging purposes? Perhaps the unpacking reveals primarily the papers of a single individual, but along with them are two small collections, the papers of two other people, which should be cataloged separately. Tentative decisions can almost always be made during the unpacking and first rough sort as to the number of cataloging units involved so that arrangement can be organized by cataloging unit from then on. Minor changes may be required later, but nine times out of ten, decisions made at this point will hold. And always remember that papers are usually together for a reason. Do not artificially create separate cataloging units. Instead, keep papers from a single source together whenever possible.

This is the time to say a word about the importance of preserving the integrity of the collections. Never should a collection be broken up or parts or items removed to place with another collection, no matter how akin the subject matter. The papers of an individual, of an institution, or of a firm must be treated as a whole, not as isolated documents, and there is no excuse for breaking the inherent unity of a collection to force its component parts into an artificial combination with some other collection or collections.

Types of Arrangement

At the same time that unboxing, cleaning and separation into cataloging units proceeds, a preliminary decision will be needed on the method or methods to use in ordering the papers. This too is a crucial decision which later will play an important role in any collection's usefulness to scholars and the ease with which it can be serviced and is another reason why these preliminary steps fall to the trained archivist or librarian rather than unskilled help.

Small collections, under two feet in size, usually shape themselves into a workable arrangement almost automatically. For letters or correspondence, a simple chronology is the obvious solution, with perhaps a separate folder or two for any miscellany such as undated speeches or genealogical materials. If the collection is composed instead of minutes, reports, or financial records, there will still be a natural inherent order functionally derived usually chronological, that the arranger can follow. Business records will fall into series, i.e., day books, ledgers, payroll records, minutes of managerial bodies, and then into chronological sequence within the series. Diaries will follow a simple chronology.

Only compilations or materials assembled by a collector will be suitable for ordering by subject. If a man's papers consist of materials he has collected on a number of Indian tribes and practices, it makes sense to keep them together by tribe or practice rather than contrive some artificial chronological ordering. In few other cases will subject ordering prove useful. Occasionally a few subject files within a collection will complement a basically chronological arrangement. If a man has assembled clippings and other materials on women's suffrage, railroad legislation, or bi-metalism, they can best be kept together by subject (as he had them) rather than be interspersed throughout chronological files. Never should an artificial subject ordering be constructed from independent collections.

The medium-sized collection of 2 - 15 feet, will usually lend itself to a similar simple chronological treatment. Personal papers, diaries, and accounts, particularly if their original order (provided there was one) has been destroyed, will take best to a time-sequence arrangement. Records of business firms and organizations or institutional archives will fall naturally into the groups or categories created as they accumulated and preservation of provenance to the extent that it can be salvaged will prove efficient in most cases.

For large collections, problems of arrangement multiply, and will absorb large amounts of staff time. Probably heaviness of use of the collection and its general importance to scholars will be primary factors in deciding how much time should be invested in its arrangement. Where original order has been preserved it will frequently prove advisable to keep it. A biographer is not seriously handicapped by such an arrangement. In fact he can work if there is no arrangement to papers at all. The casual user will find unsorted papers relatively useless, but order of provenance provided the inventorying or cataloging has been done well presents him with few problems. It may even make finding certain kinds of materials easier.

Servicing a large collection which is chronologically arranged is easier than one ordered in any other way. The untrained employee, if he knows the date of materials wanted, can remove items from a collection and return them again with accuracy and ease. The manuscript curator must decide how heavy the use of any large collection is likely to be and then weigh the cost of staff time needed for ordering it against the difficulty of servicing it if the original order is maintained. (See Chapter V).

Ordering Chronologically

It is important that the first step in the chronological ordering process be performed by a trained person. As he goes through a collection he gets the feel of the papers and the man or institution which created them. He should make notes on the order in which the papers were received if this is to be disrupted later. Occasionally a preliminary inventory will be useful. Also he is able to date with relative accuracy many undated materials, thereby preserving their usefulness and their coherence in a collection. Enclosures should be fastened to the documents with which they were enclosed. When so handled they continue to make sense and function in telling the story. Filing them under their own dates will only destroy their usefulness. At this time papers should be sorted into decades, for chronological ordering of materials of any bulk is most easily handled in a series of steps.

Once this first step is complete all further steps in a chronological arrangement can be performed by clerks. Sorting is by decades, then by year, by month and finally by day, at which time papers can be placed in their permanent folders and the folder legend typed. It is important that the quantity of materials in each folder be limited to not more than 25 items, so that if materials in a folder are disarranged they are still easily found or reordered. Larger quantities, when disarranged, result in much greater inconvenience.

The legend for each folder should include the classification number (where one is used); the name of the collection; and the dates of the papers it contains (where a strictly chronological arrangement is adhered to) or a brief description of its contents. For further identification it is wise to indicate the donor in code somewhere on the folder or document, particularly if a collection has come from several sources. The folders can then be packed in the repository's standard containers, and the containers numbered and shelved. A shelf list indicating the dates covered in each container should be prepared, and the papers are ready for cataloging.

Original Order and Order of Provenance

Provenance, as an ordering scheme, has its roots in public archives where the responsibility of the archivist to the agency creating the records makes its use imperative as well as sensible.

It stems from the origin of the papers and their original function. It does not work well with most types of personal papers. Individuals tend to live their lives chronologically. No system of arranging personal papers other than a chronological one comes as close to life as it is experienced. Institutions, however, have chronologically simultaneous functions which together make a larger and more intricate pattern. The records of an institution (be it a public agency, a business firm, a church or a social group) are most likely comprehensible only as they display their origin in the way they were originally assembled. In mid-twentieth century, individuals, especially if they are public figures, are sometimes institutional - at least in their accumulated papers, and such cases provenance will need to be respected. Provenance and original order are extremely useful in handling contemporary manuscript groups whose bulk would otherwise prove unmanageable. Provenance can always be useful when it is impossible to process a manuscript collection immediately, for if a brief preliminary inventory is prepared, the papers can be made relatively usable. Maintaining the original order of a collection as its permanent arrangement makes for quick processing. Frequently the papers can be boxed in order as they are removed from the original file drawers, kept in their original folders, and an inventory prepared which describes the characteristics of the filing system and describes which units are in each box. Usually for personal papers, original order will mean filing by name of correspondent and occasionally by subject within a period of time--sometimes a year, sometimes longer. Institutional or business records are more likely to be filed by the groups or divisions (i. e., committees, officers, departments) which created them, and then by subject or type within chronological periods. For example the records of an organization may fall into broad categories reflecting the agencies creating them such as: executive board, committees, state conventions, etc. Within these will come types of records such as minutes, reports, correspondence, mailing lists, etc. These in turn may be organized by fiscal year, biennium or perhaps longer chronological divisions.

When original order is retained, the library has several responsibilities. First it should understand the original order and be able to describe it in such a way that it is easily understood and used by the scholar. This should be done in an inventory, the preparation of which will be described in Chapter IV. Second, it must devise schemes to make it possible to remove items from the collection and return them to their proper place. With a personal filing system based on correspondents within chronological periods, this is not difficult. For an elaborate subject file, it requires more painstaking treatment. For example one library has left an elaborate collection of materials on the Philippine Islands in the order in which it was filed by the professor who assembled it. In this instance the subject headings under which he organized a vast miscellany of materials made a sensible pattern which could hardly be improved, but it did mean that each folder had to be numbered and bear the number of its box, and these folder markings must be transferred to any materials removed from a folder if they are to be returnable to their original places.

Other Ordering Schemes

Any manuscript curator or scholar who has had to cope with an undescribed but complicated ordering scheme devised (and understood) by some predecessor long since departed or dead, is aware of the pitfalls of such devices. What may have seemed like a logical system to its originator may be a Chinese puzzle to those who come after, particularly when the scheme is not adequately recorded. The simpler the arrangement, the greater its usefulness. Original order, provenance, and chronology will solve most arrangement problems.

Occasionally an attractive plea for some other arrangement scheme merits attention. Richard Berner argues strongly for a plan in which out-going letters would be arranged chronologically and incoming letters arranged alphabetically by writer (with the exception of letters written by a person acting as agent for someone else which would be filed under the latter's name). He points out that this eliminates judgment as to the importance of correspondents on the part of a cataloger since it is a matter of a moment to check whether any given person's letters appear in a collection. At the same time it provides a chronological framework from which a researcher interested in material in a certain time period can work. For the details of this approach see, Berner, Richard, "The Arrangement and Description of Manuscripts," The American Archivist, October 1960 (395-406). There are advantages to this scheme but it also increases the difficulty of locating everything that is likely to relate to a subject or occurrence in a given time period or in a specific time sequence. Imagine the difficulties in finding, for example, all materials pertaining to the election of 1932 in the thirty-year accumulation of papers of a recent political figure, if all incoming correspondence was organized alphabetically. And certainly the advantages of original order or provenance are lost, namely ease of arrangement and the natural grouping of papers which originated together. It will take as long to make this kind of arrangement, in fact longer, than a strictly chronological one.

Boxing, Labelling and Shelving

Boxing involves making a choice of containers, which in turn will be governed by the size of the collection and the amount of use. Horizontal boxes are most satisfactory for small collections and miscellaneous items. Folders and documents lie flat, and containers do not have to be completely filled to prevent warping and curling. However, they are likely to require an expensive custom order since almost all standard manuscript containers provide upright storage. If proper care is taken in packing, vertical storage will prove satisfactory. The Hollinger box is a very adequate inexpensive small container, useful for small or medium-sized collections or heavily used larger ones. Its chief disadvantage is that it comes fully assembled and thereby occupies considerable storage space before it is in use.

The most satisfactory large container is a collapsible, easily-assembled storage box which takes both regular and legal size materials and is light enough to be carried by one person. A dust proof lid and side handholds are a decided advantage. Containers larger than 12.5 x 15.5 inches are awkward to handle and any saving in money or space is offset by their inconvenience.

Labelling of all containers is of course imperative. A label is satisfactory if it tells the name of the collection, its classification number (if one is used), and the contents of the container (i.e., folder, box, or filing drawer) being labelled or its place in the order of containers, i.e., box 1, box 2, etc. Labels designed especially for the repository using them will make shelves and collections more attractive at little extra cost.

Shelving can be done in one of two ways, in order of acquisition or by a classification scheme. When shelved by the first method, each cataloging unit is assigned a number in regular progression according to the time at which it is ready to be shelved. Containers for a collection are placed on the shelves in the order determined by its arrangement, immediately behind the last collection acquired and followed by the next. There is no need to leave space for additional acquisitions, which will be handled as new collections and receive new numbers. When these numbers are placed on catalog cards, they serve to indicate a collection's location. Every inch of shelf space can be used and shelving can be acquired to meet only immediate needs. Saving of space is the chief advantage of this system.

Shelving by a classification scheme is rather more common and has decided advantages. Classification schemes for manuscript libraries are very unlike those devised for printed materials. Usually a very simple scheme which classifies collections as personal papers, church records, business records, and records of other groups and institutions will suffice. Some provision can be made for differentiating bound and unbound material or outsize items. The scheme shown in Appendix 1 has been used with success. Shelving is done in alphabetical order by collection within the classification scheme. This works very well for single items and small collections. It breaks down when very large collections must be housed because of the shifting of material that is necessary whenever a sizable acquisition is received. However, it is not hard to locate forty or fifty feet of papers and some provision for a special stack area for large collections will solve the problem.

When a classification scheme is used it must be remembered that it specifies only type of collection, i.e., personal papers, business records, institutional records, etc. It does not attempt to perform the task of the library classification scheme, which is organization according to subject matter. Manuscript collections as entities defy classification in this manner, and subject matter organization must be handled through the card catalog.

Shelving under a classification scheme permits expansion of a given collection or group of records. Additions can be made without difficulty and various sizes of bound or unbound items can be handled economically.

Summary

The most important general principle to remember in processing for a manuscript repository is to keep a balance between consistency and flexibility. Organization implies a scheme, and to attempt to deal with manuscript materials without having decided on a system for handling them would result in chaos. At the same time different kinds of materials present the curator with different kinds of problems and hence different possible solutions. A well-developed sense of order, an open mind, and a strong back are the characteristics a manuscript curator will find most helpful.

Suggested Readings for Chapter III

Donald C. Anthony, "Caring for Your Collections," American Association for State and Local History Technical Leaflet 8, History News, XVIII (April 1963).

And All the Kings Men, Lakeside Press. Chicago n.d., 42 p.

Richard C. Berner, "The Arrangement and Description of Manuscripts," The American Archivist, XVIII (October 1960), pp. 395-406.

Herman Kahn, "Librarians and Archivists--Some Aspects of Their Partnership," The American Archivist, VII (October 1944), pp. 243-251.

Lucille M. Kane, "A Guide to the Care and Administration of Manuscripts," Bulletins of the American Association for State and Local History, II (September 1960).

Robert W. Lovett, "Care and Handling of Non-Governmental Archives," Library Trends, V (January 1957), pp. 380-389.

Margaret C. Norton, "Handling Fragile Manuscripts," Illinois Libraries, XXIX (November-December 1947), pp. 410-413, 460-464.

Theodore R. Schellenberg, "Archival Principles of Arrangement," The American Archivist, XXIV (January 1961), pp. 14-24.

Theodore R. Schellenberg, "A Nationwide System of Controlling Historical Manuscripts in the United States," The American Archivist, XXVIII (July 1965), pp. 409-412.

Theodore R. Schellenberg, The Management of Archives. New York, 1965.

H. C. Schulz, "The Care and Storage of Manuscripts in the Huntington Library," Library Quarterly, V (January, 1935),

"How to Process a Manuscript Collection," Wisconsin Magazine of History, XXXVI (Spring 1953), pp. 196-197.

Chapter IV
Preparing Finding Aids

While arranging must be done from the time the first collection of any size arrives at a new manuscript library, there is a temptation to by-pass the preparation of finding aids for a while. When a library is very small, its staff members can carry in their heads enough information to make its holdings usable. Everyone knows a curator who can go directly to his shelves and pull out the papers bearing on someone's research problem or answering another's question. This kind of knowledge on the part of a library's staff will always be a useful supplement to formal finding aids, but unfortunately individuals retire, resign or die, taking their mental cataloging systems along with them. As a library increases in number of users and in holdings this reliance on personal knowledge breaks down, and the investigator is likely to miss manuscripts. Some system of information retrieval which can be made directly available to the researcher and which is based on an objective recording of the contents of collections becomes imperative, and is a primary responsibility of any manuscript repository worthy of the name. It is not enough to give safe-keeping to records and papers. They must be processed to make them usable.

Eventual multiplication of problems can be avoided if finding aids are systematically prepared from the very beginning. Without good finding aids the most meticulously arranged set of papers is only minimally useful and the most carefully acquired collection will only gather dust on the shelves. The process of preparing finding aids is far from mechanical. While staff members assigned to this task will need a large measure of those qualities associated with high level clerical skills - precision, accuracy, consistency, and attention to detail, these characteristics will not be enough. Wide familiarity with and deep understanding of the subject matter of the library's holdings and ability to empathize with the potential users of these manuscripts will also be needed. This ability to see in any set of papers the uses to which it may be put by a variety of researchers with varying interests is essential.

Selecting the Finding Aid to be Used

The calendar, the inventory and the general catalog, supplemented by shelf lists and indexes, are the most common types of finding aids. The day may come when computer information retrieval systems will be added to that list, but they are not yet serious competitors in most manuscript libraries. Which of these types you select will depend on the nature and amount of the materials your repository collects, the kinds of users it attracts, and the specific characteristics of the individual collection being processed. For example, governmental archives, because of the nature of their material and the uses they will have, depend on the inventory, equipped with its own index, as their primary and frequently their only finding aid. The manuscript library with a great preponderance of collections of personal papers will choose between the general catalog and inventory or a combination of both. The very specialized small library of rare and important documents may rely on the calendar. The finding aids or combination of finding aids to use in a given case will be delineated more sharply in the discussion of the uses and preparation of each.

The Calendar

The calendar is the oldest type of finding aid. It is also the least frequently used at present. Since it is by far the most time consuming and expensive to prepare and requires the highest level of scholarship on the part of its maker, the calendaring of papers should be considered only in very special cases. Occasionally a collection of widespread interest to scholars whose volume is small and where the usefulness of individual items lies in the ideas they express rather than in their details will be suitable for calendaring. No one should consider calendaring papers of local interest or a collection of great size where most of the individual items are of relatively slight importance. Records in which the substance consists largely of detail such as a merchant's accounts or the proceedings of a court, no matter how old or rare, are impossible to calendar in a meaningful fashion. Calendars can be particularly useful with collections of bound documents which meet the above criteria and are in no useable order, or when the papers of an individual or institution are scattered in several repositories or are in private hands.

Any calendar that is worth making at all deserves to be printed and equipped with a good index. If the calendar is to be kept on cards in the repository itself, a name index to the papers will do just as well, because a calendar's main value is to acquaint scholars with the substance of collections they may never be able to examine personally or to enable them to determine in advance, wherever they are, which items in a collection merit their further attention.

Since calendars will be infrequently prepared by the staff members of most manuscript repositories only general directions for making entries will be given here. The list of suggested readings contains references which should be carefully studied by anyone about to prepare a calendar.

The first paragraph of the entry should include the name of the sender, the place from which it was written or dispatched and the name of the recipient and its destination. The date of the document should appear directly opposite this in the left hand margin and its number in the collection on the right hand margin. The second paragraph contains the abstract of its contents. No matter how many ideas or subjects the letter or document includes, only one paragraph should be used, with the order of ideas following that of the original and each subject or thought separated by semicolons. The next paragraph will state via abbreviations what type of paper it is (document, letter, draft, or copy), if it is autograph or typescript, whether it is signed, and if it was or had an enclosure. Enclosures are always treated as separate documents. The last paragraph when needed will contain lists of names or places mentioned if these have not been included in the abstract itself. Below is an example of an entry in the calendar of the

James Burrill Angell Papers:

Sept 3, 1869	E.C. Walker, Detroit to James B. Angell, Vermont University. Invites Angell to accept the presidency of The University of Michigan; explains the presidency was first offered to J.H. Seelye of Amherst who suggested Angell; salary mentioned. A. L. S.	No. 79

Indexing should be done to the number of the calendar entry rather than to the printed page so that it can be prepared before the calendar is set in proof.

The Inventory

The inventory grew out of the needs for servicing governmental archives. The science of archival management as we know it originated in Europe and was fathered in this country by the National Archives, where inventorying the vast collections of federal records has been brought to a science. The preparation of inventories for governmental records will not be discussed in this volume. The reader is referred instead to T. R. Schellenberg's Modern Archives and The Management of Archives, and urged to study as the best examples of the craft in English the published inventories of the National Archives.

When an inventory is prepared for personal papers it begins with a page or two of description of a collection as a whole and biographical data on the individual or family who accumulated the papers. A genealogical chart will also be helpful. This will be followed by a brief description of the way the manuscripts are organized, and a list by box or folder number of the various groups (or series) of papers within the collection. Following this each group or series is described individually. Subjects discussed, names of correspondents and recipients, places from which letters or other documents originated, are brought out in these descriptions. Careful indexing, especially of the series descriptions, is essential to make the inventory useful. If the maker of the inventory has done his job well the index will permit the researcher to tell at a glance if a collection contains material on his subject or letters to or from individuals in whom he is interested.

Inventories of institutional or organizational records will follow a similar pattern. First there will be a general description of the papers including material on the history of the business firm, church body, or professional organization whose records are being described. Again structural charts for various periods of the organization's development will be useful. This general description will be followed by a simple list of the various series or groups of records which compose the collection, and this in turn will be followed by the more detailed descriptions of these groups. As with personal papers, an index is essential to the usefulness of the inventory.

One great advantage of the inventory is that it can be printed to facilitate wide circulation among scholars and libraries. A disadvantage is that each index to each collection must be consulted individually to assess the holdings of any one institution that are pertinent to any given subject or individual. As the number of collections for which a repository has inventories increases, this task can assume formidable proportions.

When is it appropriate to make an inventory? Obviously this is far too pretentious a device to be practical for single items or small collections. It would be preposterous to prepare an inventory to a ten item collection and even more ridiculous to publish it. However the inventory is almost the only manageable finding aid for the large collection of twenty-five to a thousand or more linear feet. Large collections almost inevitably fall into groups or series which can be described individually. Their physical bulk makes it impossible to indicate the nature of their contents item by item. And occasionally they will be of sufficient interest to warrant the expense of publishing a finding aid to a single collection. In short, bulky collections of personal papers and institutional or organizational records will be suitable for inventorying.

The inventory is also the most satisfactory form of finding aid for collections to which regular additions are being made. Manuscript repositories collecting contemporary papers of persons, organizations, or institutions will find it an indispensable tool, because it is a simple matter to add descriptions of new groups of papers to an existing inventory as they arrive. For contemporary or incomplete collections which are temporarily closed to use the inventory should be kept as brief as possible, serving more as a preliminary check list to indicate the location of material if the donor needs access to it. Occasionally an invoice which is complete enough to form the basis of its inventory will accompany a collection. Inventories of incomplete collections should not be published, and there is no need to index inventories to closed collections until such time as they are about to be opened for public use.

The General Catalog

Most manuscript libraries will find the general catalog their most efficient finding aid. The catalog will need to be supplemented by calendars or inventories to certain collections, but it is the only manageable scheme for retaining complete control over a large number of collections which vary widely in size, importance, and subject matter coverage. The skills used in preparing cards for a general catalog and even the procedures followed are not very different from those used in the preparation of an inventory. The information gathered by the cataloger will be much the same. Only the way in which it will be made available to the researcher will be different.

After a collection is sorted, arranged and boxed, it should be read by a member of the staff with adequate training (usually at the graduate level) in the subject fields in which the library collects. In the course of this reading, cataloging notes of several types should be made. First the reader should be alert for subject references, and should indicate where, in any given set of papers, material on any subject can be found. He should also indicate something of its nature. The subject heading list used will vary from library to library depending on the nature of the materials in its collections and the areas in which it has resources. Each repository must develop its own list and follow it to insure consistency in cataloging entries. The cataloger should note material which fits under place names, for example the residence of the originator of the papers or of his frequent correspondents, or descriptions of communities or geographical features at various points in time.

Perhaps most important for his notes, the cataloger will compile a selected list of correspondents, noting the dates and sometimes the subject of individual letters when the subject occurs rarely in a collection; or inclusive dates and general subject coverage if the papers include a large body of such correspondence. It is here that the cataloger's broad familiarity with the area of interest in which his library has materials is most essential and where thorough training in the appropriate academic discipline plays the most crucial role. There are dangers, of course, in making a select list of names as against a complete name index; its usefulness is dependent on the cataloger's wide acquaintance with the names that merit mention. But the saving in time where staff resources are limited warrants this risk. This list of correspondents should be supplemented by noting the names of persons about whom there is significant material in the collection but no letters written by them.

When these notes are transferred to catalog cards the emphasis will be on bringing out correspondents, subjects and place names on added entry cards and limiting the main card to a general description of the papers. Unlike the standard library card for printed materials, the added entry cards need not repeat the full description of the papers which appears on the main card. When the list of added entries is too long to fit on the back of a single card, additional cards may be used or the added entry list may be kept with the shelf list or the papers themselves and this fact noted on the back of the main card. Added entry headings for materials about something or someone are made in red. When the added entry is the name of a person who has authored letters or other material in a collection it appears in black. When these cards are filed in the catalog black cards precede the red and the user can tell at a glance which materials a man has written and which only contain references to him.

The great advantage of the general catalog is that it works

equally well for a collection of 800 feet or a single item. The larger collection will need a larger number of added entry cards and will take much longer to catalog than the single letter, which will need only a card or two, but the same methods are equally appropriate for both. The user will find in a single catalog under the names of persons, places, organizations or subjects, those collections which contain material pertinent for his research and usually a cue about the exact location of a document in a given collection and possibly a word or two on the nature of its contents.

Both notes and catalog cards can be best illustrated by the following example of actual notes as they were taken during the reading of the papers of Henry Howland Crapo, land speculator, lumberman, and governor of Michigan, 1865-1868, and the catalog cards which were made from these notes. (A copy of the Shelf List for the Crapo Papers appears in Appendix 2) The numbers in the right hand corner of the cards indicate the donors of this particular collection. The classification symbol for unbound personal papers appears in the left hand margin opposite the name of the assembler of the collection.

Example of Rough Notes

Giddings, Orrin N , 1814-
several letters, 1854, 1855, 1856, 1857, mostly about land purchases

Williams, Harvey, 1812-1867 of Eaton County
letters, 1854, 1855, 1856, mostly about land

Railroads
material on railroad bill vetoes in 1867

Railroads
Oakland and Ottawa RR described in letter Dec. 28, 1854, WWC to HHC

Railroads
descrip. Lansing and Saginaw RR, March 26, 1856

Railroads
material on Flint and Holy RR, Aug. 30, Nov. 23, Dec. 1862; 1863, 1864, Jan. 21, 1867.

If rough notes are made on 3 x 5-inch slips, those pertaining to a single individual, place, or subject can be more easily put together later on a single added entry card. Noting the date of a letter (or the years when a large body of correspondence from a single individual or on a single subject appears) makes it easier for the researcher to judge if it will be useful to him and also easier for the staff member to locate.

Examples of Catalog Cards

Main card for the collection

```
                                                        1060
                                                          11
Ab  Crapo, Henry Howland, 1804-1869.
      Papers, 1830-1920, of Henry Howland Crapo and
    the Crapo family, including correspondence dealing
    with Crapo's land sepculations, lumbering, and politi-
    cal activities in great detail, and correspondence of
    his son re his estate and land holdings after his death;
    speeches, notes and other papers dealing with the gov-
    ernorship; deeds and other papers dealing with his
    land purchases in Ohio, Iowa, and Michigan; clippings,
    biographical material, obituaries; personal and busi-
    ness accounts; receipts and vouchers. [see shelf list]
      32 boxes
```

Back of main card showing partial added entry list

Adrian, Mich.	Election of 1864
Agriculture	Election of 1866
Aldrich, Nelson W	Election of 1888
Bacon, Daniel S	Fairfield, Mich.
Baker, Orrin	Fenton, Wm. M
Cass, Lewis	Flint, Mich.
Christiancy, Isaac P	Flint and Holly Railroad
Civil War	Giddings, Orrin N
Crapo, David	Gilman, Daniel Coit
Driggs, John F	Michigan. Governor
Duffield, D. Bethune	Green, Noah H
Election of 1862	Isle Royale Mining Co.
	(con't on next card)

Giddings, Orrin N 1814- 1060
Ab Crapo, Henry Howland, 1804-1869. 11
Papers, 1830-1920, of Henry Howland Crapo and the Crapo family, including several letters, 1854-1857, and one Jan. 19, 1867, from Orrin Giddings, mostly dealing with land matters.
32 boxes

Added entry card for correspondent

in red--

1060
Adrian, Mich. 11
Ab Crapo, Henry Howland, 1804-1869.
Papers, 1830-1920, of Henry Howland Crapo and the Crapo family, including a letter of August 16, 1847, about a cholera epidemic in Adrian, also letters, 1853, written by Crapo to his son and dated from Adrian with some comments on the community.
32 boxes

Added entry card for a place name

1060
11
Railroads. --in red
Ab Crapo, Henry Howland, 1804-1869.
Papers, 1830-1920, of Henry Howland Crapo and the Crapo family, including considerable correspondence and other papers dealing with Michigan railroads, among them the Oakland and Ottawa Railroad, described in a letter of Dec. 28, 1854; Lansing and Saginaw Railroad, Mar. 26,1856; material on the Flint and Holly and the Flint and Pere Marquette; also papers and correspondence re Crapo's vetoes of the railroad acts during his governorship.
32 boxes

Added entry card for a subject

When these cataloging techniques are carried out properly, any user should be able to look in the general catalog of a repository under a man's name and by simply thumbing through the cards learn how many of his letters it has, from which periods of his career they come, and in what collections they are located. A glance at the catalog under a place name should show what business records, church and organization records, personal papers, diaries, etc., originated in that place or contain materials pertaining to it. Subject heading entries should give a complete picture of the library's holdings which bear on some area of subject matter.

The features of the inventory and the general catalog can be combined for large collections by making two sets of notes simultaneously. Along with the cataloging notes described above which will be transferred to the catalog cards themselves, the cataloger should be making a running description of the papers. This description should be much more detailed than the one appearing on the main catalog card, and will be organized by group into which the papers fall, indicating the contents and scope of each group and the principal correspondents therein. Later a general description of the papers will be written to preface the running description, and biographical and genealogical data will be added. In most cases this inventory or description can be combined with the shelf list and either placed with the papers themselves or filed in some convenient spot from which it can be made available to investigators. Copies can be made of this inventory shelf list for personal use by investigators. On those rare occasions when the importance of a collection warrants publishing a formal inventory, the inventory-shelf list described above will serve as its basis. In general the publication budgets of manuscript libraries can be better spent in preparing guides to the library's full holdings rather than on publishing inventories to individual collections. Examples of descriptive inventory-shelf lists appear in Appendix 2.

Special Indexes

A good index is required to make a calendar or inventory useful, as has been pointed out above. Essentially, the general catalog is no more than a master name and subject index to all of a library's holdings. However there may be occasions when the staff time needed to make a complete name index to an individual collection will be justified. This deserves consideration if a collection will receive very heavy casual use, by which we mean that scholars, students and others will be widely interested in the letters written by the correspondents of the person whose papers these are. The volume of this interest may be larger than interest in the career of the person himself. It also precludes a high proportion of significant figures among his correspondents. Rarely should a complete name index for a collection be attempted if its preparation means that large quantities of other material will be left unprocessed and uncataloged.

A name index is easy to prepare and can be done by less highly skilled persons than are required for selective cataloging. Since it must be combined with selective cataloging, especially for subject entries, the papers will still have to be read by the skilled cataloger, resulting in no real saving of high level staff time. In making a name index the correspondence files are examined item by item and the name of the correspondent, the date of the letter, and occasionally a word about its subject or an indication of its location (if materials are not arranged chronoligically) are transferred to 3 x 5 inch cards. All card pertaining to correspondence with a single person are eventually put in chronological order and combined on one card which looks like this:

Johnson, Lyndon Baines, 1908-
Jan. 4, 1958 (congratulatory)
March 21, 1960 (re oil legislation)
Sept. 10, 1962 (in public works file)

Name Index Card

Every correspondent, regardless of his importance, receives such a card, and every communication, no matter how minor, is duly noted. In addition cards referring users to the name index will be put in the general catalog for important correspondents, as below:

Johnson, Lyndon Baines, Pres. U. S., 1908-
Aa Williams, Gerhard Mennen, 1911-
Papers, 1930-1963, of G. Mennen Williams, Governor of Michigan and Secretary of State for African Affairs, including correspondence with Lyndon B. Johnson. [See name index and inventory to Williams papers.]
982 ft.

Scrapbooks are also suitably indexed individually. While they may not merit item-by-item treatment, some form of guide will vastly increase their usefulness. Frequently they contain correspondence, clippings, programs, and other memorabilia which pertains to organizations, occasions, or individuals quite unrelated to their compiler. Indexes can be prepared by relatively unskilled help or the information can be compiled on guide forms of the sort found in Appendix 3.

The Chronological Catalog

A chronological catalog by decades or half decades is very simple to prepare and makes an excellent supplementary finding aid. At the time the main card is made for the general catalog, cards which repeat the information on the main card also are made under the proper chronological divisions, filed in drawers in chronological order, and by alphabet within the chronology. The researcher looking for materials on a certain period will find this file most helpful in checking whether or not he has completely exhausted possible sources. Its preparation is a purely mechanical task which can be performed by clerical staff.

	1060	
1835-1839	11	date in red
Ab Crapo, Henry Howland, 1804-1869. Papers, 1830-1920, of Henry Howland Crapo and the Crapo family, including correspondence dealing with Crapo's land speculations, lumbering, and political activities in great detail, and correspondence of his son re his estate and land holdings after his death; speeches, notes and other papers dealing with the governorship; deeds and other papers dealing with his land purchases in Ohio, Iowa, and Mich; clippings, biographical material, obituaries; personal and business accounts; receipts and vouchers. [See shelf list.] 32 boxes		

Card for Chronological Catalog

Cataloging Microfilms, Pictures, Maps, and Printed Materials

Microfilms should be cataloged exactly the same way as would be the originals from which they were made, and the necessary cards should be similarly filed in the appropriate catalog. The same classification system should be used except that the fact that they are microfilm should appear under the classification designation. In short, microfilms should be read, the appropriate notes taken, main cards and added entry cards prepared, and when size and importance of materials merit it, a descriptive inventory prepared. The location of the original and whether the film is negative or positive should also be noted on the cards.

Pictures pose more of a problem. They will come in every size, shape, and condition. Some will be an integral part of the collection they accompany; others will supplement some other phase of a library's holdings. Two things can be done with them. They can be kept as a part of the papers with which they arrived and cataloged as part of that collection in the same way the rest of it is being handled; or they can be treated as separate units for cataloging purposes. When pictures have little independent value and are useful chiefly to supplement a collection they should be kept

	1771
Aa Micro	Van Raalte, Albertus Augustus, 1811-1876. Papers, 1840-1847, of Albertus Van Raalte, minister of Holland, Mich; correspondence, deeds, land grants, etc., dealing with Van Raalte and the Dutch settlers of Holland. Negative. [Original papers in Calvin College Library, Grand Rapids, Mich]. (See calendar to film in Aa Van Raalte.) 3 reels

Card for a collection on microfilm

with the collection. For example, pictures of African natives made by an anthropologist and given to a library with his papers, should stay with those papers if the focus of the repository is not African ethnology but Michigan and Michigan men. Anyone interested in anthropological data using such a library should expect to find pertinent materials in the anthropologist's papers and not in any other part of the library.

However most manuscript libraries will find they have many calls for pictorial materials quite apart from the normal research based on their manuscripts. Ours is an age in which the visual is emphasized. The press and the television producer are in constant need of pictorial material. Authors of books need illustrations. A picture file, independent of holdings, will be much easier to service and can be much more easily indexed. In most cases little damage will be done to a collection if pictures which are pertinent to the library's holdings are removed from it and handled independently.

The classification scheme under which pictures are filed can closely parallel that used for manuscripts (see Appendix 1), except that categories indicating size will become more important. A name index should be made for all pictures of individuals. Pictures of geographical features can be filed under place names, and pictures of subject interest on such topics as mining, paper manufacturing, or domestic architecture, should be filed under the proper subject. Some cross-referencing will be desirable since the picture of a man's house may belong with photographs of him and his family but also have interest for the seeker of Greek Revival houses built in the 1830's. However, if all pictures are equipped with index cards which note their content and location, added entry cards can be made where a single picture fits under more than one entry. The whole picture index can be filed in a single alphabet.

	Angell, James Burrill
UA_s	Daguerreotype and 22 other individual pictures
UBI_{mu} B2	With University of Michigan faculty, 1880
UBI_{mu} E25	With Medical faculty, 1879
E1	exercises at University Hall on unveiling of Angell portrait.

Picture Index Card

Maps will also need a separate index. Most of them will be printed but manuscript maps should be treated similarly. Each map has its own card which should include the following information: area mapped, maker, publisher and engraver (if printed), date, scale, size, and number and subject of insets if any. These cards will be filed first under place name and then in chronological order.

When a printed collection is acquired to supplement the holdings of a manuscript library, it should be cataloged separately according to standard library procedure, using Library of Congress cards when these are available. Application, when possible, of the same categories of added entries as are found in the manuscript catalog will increase its usefulness. Printed materials that are an integral part of manuscript collections, such as pamphlet materials in red--

Michigan. Lower Peninsula. MB. 3 Map of the southern part of Michigan, by John Farmer. Published by J. H. Colton and Co. New York, 1857. Engraved by S. Stiles & Co. New York. Entered... in the Year 1855 by J. H. Colton & Co... in New York. 23 x 33 inches. Three insets (1) Northern part of Michigan. (2) Map of Mackinaw Isle. Scale 2 miles to an inch. (3) Map of the Straits of Mackinaw. From actual survey. Scale ca. 5 miles to an inch. Karpinski no. 198.

Card for a Map

acquired by a politician at various phases of his career, or clippings collected by a statesman or scholar should be treated as manuscript material and left with the collector's other papers.

Mechanized Information Retrieval Systems

The key punch, the sorter, the computer or some uninvented supermachine may some day make obsolete all the above pages on the preparation of finding aids. In fact it is already technically possible to completely mechanize finding devices. Why then plod along with human catalogers and retrievers in this automated age? First and foremost, because the devising and installation of any information retrieval system adequate to serve a manuscript library would, under present conditions, be far more expensive than the cost of hiring human beings to do the job. Mechanization can be used effectively in certain highly specialized situations. There is too little call for most material in the average manuscript library to warrant the cost of processing each item, to say nothing of the degree of care and skill needed to devise coding systems to cope adequately with the almost endless stream of uses to which manuscript material can be put, and no amount of mechanization will retrieve anything which has been misindexed or miscoded. As of this writing, manpower and money can be used more efficiently in traditional methods of arranging and cataloging. However many of the finding devices described here, i. e., name indexes, subject and place name headings in catalogs, could be used as the basis for mechanization without losing the initial cataloging effort.

Summary

The holdings of a manuscript repository are useful to the scholar only to the extent that he knows what they contain and can efficiently gain access to those papers which are pertinent to his problem. The calendar, the complete name index, or the inventory are all useful finding aids in certain situations and for certain types of collections. However, most manuscript libraries will find that a general catalog plus a chronological catalog when combined with inventories and shelf lists for larger collections will give them most effective control over their collections and will be their most satisfactory finding aid. The general catalog should receive the largest expenditure of staff time and skill. Similar cataloging procedures will provide control over microfilms, pictures, maps, and printed materials which supplement the manuscript collections.

Of course, few manuscript libraries will be able to realize the ideal of having their resources adequately cataloged or otherwise provided with suitable finding aids. Some collections will of necessity have to be inadequately cataloged or not cataloged at all except for a single card containing a brief description of the papers waiting for a happier day when staff time is available to do a thorough job. In such cases a certain amount of informal passing on of information by staff members to users will help to bridge the gap. Also the mature scholare will never be completely dependent on finding aids although they can vastly simplify his task. In general, the usefulness of collections will depend on the degree to which good finding aids have been prepared. No other aspect of a library's activities is more deserving of staff time or more dependent on a high level of staff skill.

Suggested Readings

Hermione M. Baumhoffer, "Film Records Management," _The American Archivist_, XIX (July 1956), pp. 235-248.

Francis Bello, "How to Cope with Information," _Fortune,_ LXII (September 1960), pp. 162-167, 180, 182.

Richard C. Berner, "Archivists, Librarians, and the National Union Catalog of Manuscript Collections," The American Archivist, XXVII (July 1964), pp. 401-409.

William H. Bond, "The Cataloging of Manuscripts in the Houghton Library," Harvard Library Bulletin, IV (Autumn 1950), pp. 392-396.

Ruth Bordin, "Michigan - The G. Mennen Williams Papers," The American Archivist, XXVI (July 1963), pp. 345-354.

Lucille M. Kane, "A Guide to the Care and Administration of Manuscripts," Bulletins of the American Association for State and Local History, II (September 1960).

Clyde M. Coller, "The Archivist and Weather Records," The American Archivist, XXVI (October 1963), pp. 477-485.

Paul S. Dunkin, "Arrangement and Cataloging of Manuscripts," Library Trends, V (January 1957), pp. 352-360.

Robert A. Fairthorne, Towards Information Retrieval. London 1961.

J. C. Fitzpatrick, Notes on the Care, Cataloguing, Calendaring, and Arrangement of Manuscripts. Washington. 1934 Edition.

Worthington C. Ford, "On Calendaring Manuscripts," Papers of the Bibliographical Society of America, IV (1909), pp. 45-46.

Richard W. Hale, "The Cataloging of Microfilm," The American Archivist, XXII (January 1959), pp. 11-13.

Evelyn Hensel, "Treatment of Non-Book Materials," Library Trends, II (October 1953), pp. 187-198.

Howard Peckham, "Arranging and Cataloging Manuscripts in the William L. Clements Library," The American Archivist, I (October 1938), pp. 215-229.

Morris L. Radoff, "A Guide to Practical Calendaring," The American Archivist, XI (April 1948), pp. 123-140; XII (July 1948), pp. 203-222.

Theodore R. Schellenberg, Modern Archives. Chicago 1956.

Theodore R. Schellenberg, The Management of Archives, New York 1965.

Brian Campbell Vickery, On Retrieval System Theory. London 1961.

Chapter V

Problems with Contemporary Papers

The primary physical characteristic of contemporary papers whether those of an individual or an institution is their bulk. Everyone is aware of the accelerating rate at which man has produced paper artifacts in the twentieth century, but no one knows this better than the archivist or librarian who must cope with permanent storage of this never ending stream of holograph, typewritten, mimeographed, filmed, near-printed, and published material. It seems unlikely that ever again will the lifetime accumulation of papers of a public figure be adequately shelved in thirty cubic feet of space.

The nature of personal papers has also changed drastically. Instead of several richly informative personal diaries, a few volumes of letterpress books, and a modest file of holograph letters from friends, family, and associates, typical of the 19th century public leader, a contemporary official is more likely to produce 800 feet of records: correspondence, incoming and outgoing (not infrequently in triplicate); appointment books and schedules, recordings of speeches, motion picture films of public appearances; mimeographed copies of reports, speeches, and press releases (often multi-copies); the papers of all his aides and secretaries and their memoranda to him--in short a room full of documents, some as meaningful and rich in research potential as those of his earlier counterpart but many (usually those which occupy the most space) of relatively little value.

Problems of Selection

Obviously twentieth century America cannot preserve all its paper. Were it to attempt to do so a great share of society's human and physical resources eventually would be needed to care for and store it. Society is unlikely to view preserving records as one of its major functions. What is the answer to all this bulk? Should we microfilm routinely, destroy the originals, and keep instead the antiseptic, space-saving films in their compact storage bins? Few scholars would urge such drastic measures and most administrators are aware that this too is a costly business. Nor does it solve the scholar's problem of how to encompass this mass of paper and incorporate it into his research. Printed materials alone for current history are so vast that if we confront the scholar with a mass of unselected manuscript as well, he is likely to bypass manuscript resources entirely. Those whose responsibility it is to decide on what is to be kept in this age of the abundance of paper must take care to be discriminating, must practice much more selectivity than was necessary in the past.

While selection necessarily plays a role in all collecting, it becomes much more important and more difficult when dealing with contemporary papers. Selection, by its very nature, not only solves problems but creates a whole new roster of problems. The questions of what to save and how long to save it take on special significance when asked in connection with contemporary records. We understand what records of a hundred years ago merit keeping. We can assess the importance of correspondents; we know which movements played a crucial role in the American scene. When we relegate things to the trash barrel we can have some confidence in our judgment. The problem is of a different nature when we move into the records of the mid-twentieth century. Recent personal papers are frequently those of living persons, sometimes men or women whose active careers are still in mid-stream. Other collections are those of people only lately retired or deceased. Can the manuscript repository receiving the papers of a current Congressman afford to practice selection, or even obtain his permission to practice it, on records which he himself may still have to use? Equally important, can the archivist or librarian assess the eventual importance of the public figure himself? Also, what of the people who make up his correspondents, his aides, even his constituents? Many of them are young. Who knows but what several embryonic public figures whose careers may easily outdistance his own are among them.

Such are the arguments for accepting and storing contemporary papers in their totality, leaving the weeding process to future generations. These arguments are not without merit. Perhaps they shift the selection process from emphasis on what papers of an individual or institution ought to be saved to the selection of those individuals or institutions important enough to merit preservation of their papers. But there can be hazards in this solution too. Future generations can assess the value of a man quite differently than do his contemporaries, and the embryonic stages of movements under such a system would go unnoticed and unrecorded.

One has to select, for the problem of bulk cannot be ignored, yet one cannot arrive at a logical, foolproof set of rules which will serve as an adequate guide in performing the selection function. Rule of thumb, intuition, and arbitrary decision will no doubt prove the most useful hand-maidens in the process. Rule of thumb tells you that correspondence and other papers relating to the policy-making process are important. Those which record mere administrative routines are not. It also suggests that one can afford to destroy duplicates provided they are really duplicates and not drafts. It indicates that only samples of form letters (with perhaps lists of names of people to whom they were sent) are important. It suggests that if accounts are carefully and fully entered in a formal ledger, there is no need to preserve the bank checks, bills, receipts and vouchers which make up the bulk of financial records. Certainly if the book and pamphlet material which a man gathered and scattered throughout his papers is readily available in any good public library, a list of what he owned can take the place of the physical presence of his books. These are examples of clear-cut cases.

But what of the letters on pending legislation to a governor from his constituents? Should 4000 almost identical letters from farmers and others in favor of a milk-dating bill all be kept? Representative sampling is a possible answer; the saving of every tenth letter, which should give an adequate feel for the range of sentiment and the kind of person who wrote on a given issue. In many ways this is the most intelligent approach for it bases the selection process on a purely objective criterion, unbiased by human judgment. In any large collection there will be many occasions for this type of decision. Letters from constituents is only one example. Christmas cards, requests for gifts or souvenirs, routine complaints, requests for messages of greeting, can all be treated the same way.

Any form of selection takes time. In order to select, the manuscript librarian must look at the papers in detail. Only the professionally trained person can make an intelligent judgment; and as pointed out above, this is increasingly difficult as the papers approach the present time. While it seems safe enough to discard duplicates immediately, perhaps representative sampling belongs on a time schedule--a ritual to be performed ten years, twenty-five years or fifty years after deposit. There is no easy answer. Each responsible curator, archivist and librarian will have to work out his own solutions, and each in turn will probably solve the problem slightly differently with each collection he handles.

Problems of Arrangment

The arrangement of contemporary papers also presents special problems. From one point of view it might be said instead that contemporary papers present no problems, for in practice the curator is faced with little choice. Nine times out of ten, time, money, staff will require that the large collection of recent papers be left in the order in which they are received. A cursory inventory is made, a card or two of general description is placed in the manuscript catalog and from there on the researcher is on his own. But whenever this is done, and whoever does it, sees this as sheer expediency, and expects to move as rapidly as possible toward more permanent processing. Nonetheless there is much to be said for holding to provenance in ordering recent papers. In the case of individuals who are still living, the filing system which they (or more likely their secretaries) set up, remains undisturbed and makes for easy access to any information or materials which they themselves may need. The same holds true for the papers and records of continuing organizations, be they business firms, churches, social or professional groups. Contemporary records almost always arrive in installments as files are retired and until complete no other order than provenance can make sense or have permanence. When kept in their original order, cataloging can be kept to a minimum, an inventory taking the place of detailed examination or indexing, and additions made to a collection as further papers are deposited. This system has been used to advantage at The University of Michigan with the papers of recent governors. In the case of G. Mennen Williams most of the papers were opened to researchers by the retiring governor and hence had to be made available to scholars as quickly as possible. A detailed inventory combined with a complete name index made in the Governor's office as a finding device for his own secretarial staff made it possible to find quickly almost any needed materials, including single items. In this case, however, more than cursory cataloging was attempted and cards were placed in the general manuscript catalog for all of his correspondents of national and international importance as well as for less obvious subject entries. The rationale was that any scholar or student working on some phase of Michigan history or life for the twelve year period of Williams' incumbency (1949-1960) would undoubtedly be sent to his papers. It was to inform the potential casual and incidental user of these papers, that they were cataloged. Another recent gubernatorial collection was indefinitely closed by the donor when deposited. While an inventory was made primarily to assist in servicing the donor's requests, there was no attempt to catalog the collection, and only a main card was placed in the catalog. In this case no name index came with the papers.

Occasionally it will be profitable to treat a collection in some other way, especially if the collection is complete and the donor deceased. A recent collection of considerable size--135 feet of the papers of a mid-twentieth century governor, federal supreme court justice, and cabinet member was recently acquired by The University of Michigan from several sources. The papers covered all aspects of his life. Many of the files, for example those dealing with Supreme Court cases, arrived in excellent order, were kept intact, and inventories prepared for them. The correspondence, newspaper clippings, etc. were in only partial order, and the decision was made to sort all of these materials chronologically. A complete correspondent index was made for both the files left in original order and those chronologically sorted. The cost of this processing in staff time was great, but it was expected that this would be the most heavily used collection in the library. Because of the thorough ness with which finding aids were prepared and arrangement was done, servicing will be relatively simple and scholars will be able to use the material efficiently. What would have been a wasteful and extravagant treatment for a less important, less used collection, should prove economical in the long run in this case.

There are no standard solutions to arrangement problems. Despite the merits of consistency, each case will require a decision based on what is the best solution for that particular collection. The solution will depend on accessibility, usefulness of existing order, completeness of the collection, and potential intensity of its use.

Problems of Access

The administrator of a manuscript repository is never faced with more critical decisions than those surrounding access to recent or contemporary papers. The old rule, that the historian has both right and duty to examine all materials pertinent to his problem, works very well when the matters under scrutiny belong to the past. It leads only to trouble if applied to contemporary and recent history As T.R. Schellenberg has said, "By being too hasty in opening records for public use the archivist and, parenthetically, the historian may defeat their purpose of promoting objective research." (T.R. Schellenberg, Modern Archives, 266) To the question, why cannot all papers be made available to all scholars who wish to use them, Herman Kahn, then director of the Roosevelt Library at Hyde Park, has answered:

> The fact that this question is raised at all seems to be an indication that historians in this country have never faced up to the full implications, for their techniques and research methods, of the current fashion of attempting to write definitive histories of what happened in the

very recent past" (Kahn, Herman, "World War II and its Background: Research materials at the Franklin D. Roosevelt Library and policies concerning their use," _The American Archivist_, XVII:2 (April 1954, 160).

Although it is the responsibility of the manuscript library to keep limitations at a minimum, the larger interests of scholarship cannot be served by indiscriminate access to contemporary papers. To the extent that such access runs the risk of damaging living persons, exposing to public view communications and revelations made in complete confidence, it can by its very nature undermine the trust which men place in their officials. It can destroy the willingness of public figures to record their actions. It can negate an advisor's willingness to contribute to a statesman his knowledge and advice.

The easiest way to handle the problem of access would be simply to close all personal papers until such time as their use could not conceivably do harm to any living person or to the national security. This, of course, is much too drastic a solution and no responsible library would consider applying it indiscriminately, even though there may be single collections for which it must be done.

Donor-imposed restrictions are of course the easiest to administer, and the temptation to encourage this form of control is great. If the donor is liberal in his provisions, the library can blame any awkwardness on the donor's imprudence. If he has been unduly cautious, perhaps closing the collection completely, the library staff has a perfect excuse. Donors are not, however, the best judges of what should or should not be open. The trained library staff member, with his varied experience, is in a much better position to make such decisions and should not abdicate his responsibility. The donor's wishes will have to be respected, but the responsible administrator will make every effort to influence and guide him.

The Presidential Libraries have adopted the policy of removing from any collection, subject to periodic review, all purely financial and personal records of living persons or any materials which could personally injure living persons or harm the national interest. This is a sensible rule that other repositories could well follow. A corollary that assures further safeguards is to stipulate that recent and contemporary collections are open only to scholars (or graduate students working under the immediate supervision of such a scholar) for serious research. Thus the newspaper reporter, the magazine feature writer and the political enemy, whose interests are personal profit rather than the service of history, are automatically barred. They can look to other sources for their materials.

Problems of Servicing

Good finding aids will help in all servicing problems. But servicing does not stop once the scholar has in his hands the material he wishes to use. Within the hour the researcher will be inquiring about microfilming or other forms of duplication. Here the manuscript librarian's problems really begin. Once it is duplicated, the library essentially loses control of its material, and techniques must be developed to provide for continuing control. This problem and solutions to it will be dealt with in more detail in Chapter VIII. However, it should be pointed out that embarassing use of material is much more likely with recent collections, and restrictions on quotation, literary rights, requirements for proper citation, are essential.

In any case, the mechanical problems in providing duplicating services for contemporary and recent collections are formidable. Only minor use of staff time is involved in replacing a few items removed from a single box or two of 19th century papers, but the researcher who removes from a large and carefully arranged set of papers, a hundred items that he wishes placed on microfilm may cost the library twenty hours of staff time before they are restored to their proper places. This problem can become almost insuperable with papers left in original order, especially if the researcher independently begins his selection process before the staff can note the folders from which his precious finds are taken. And the researcher will do just this, unless properly warned and supervised from the day he first sets foot in the library.

Permitting filming by unit (i.e., a folder, a Hollinger box, or a unit of time if papers are chronologically arranged) eliminates this difficulty. The expense to the researcher is greater, but the cost to the library is much less.

Literary Rights

Papers are property. As such they can be physically disposed of as their owner sees fit. However under common law the literary rights, including the right of first publication, do not automatically accompany the manuscript which is donated or sold, but must be disposed of separately. At this writing (1965) literary rights in manuscripts are protected only by common law, not U.S. copyright. The proposed new copyright law (1965) would include manuscripts, and extend to them the same protection given to printed materials, the author's lifetime plus fifty years. With contemporary papers the problems attendant on this legal fact take on another dimension, for frequently nearly all a man's correspondents will still be alive. Under law, unless they have individually waived their literary property rights, the letters they wrote or the memos they dictated cannot be quoted or reproduced. While the donor of these papers may have transferred his own literary property rights to the repository, he never possessed the power to transfer those of other persons. Obviously the library cannot assume the responsibility of clearing rights or giving permission. This is the user's sole responsibility but he should be warned of his obligations.

Is warning him enough? Does the library have a further responsibility to protect the scholar from possible error of omission and its embarassing consequences by prohibiting duplication of recent materials? The Library of Congress obviously feels that it does, for it refuses to photocopy recent manuscripts without specific permission from the writer of the manuscript (or his heirs) unless these literary rights have been specifically dedicated to the public. The Presidential Libraries have provided in their deed of gift for the reversion of literary rights after the death of the donor of papers to the library itself. While this makes clear the status of those papers for which the donor can claim authorship, it does not provide for the literary rights attached to papers within a collection authored by other persons. Careful warning of users coupled with caution in permitting duplication is the only answer to this knotty problem. Caution cannot be overdone.

Summary

Increasingly the library which has specialized in the history of a region or clustered its materials around a movement or subject, painstakingly gathering the fragmentary records of the past, is confronted with a major contemporary collection. We have attempted to treat briefly some of the problems which inevitably arrive with the papers, revolving around selction, arrangement, access, servicing, and legal rights. Answers to these problems are yet to be fully worked out. Solutions are partial and frequently characterized by expediency, but facing the problems cannot be avoided. Only by looking at them squarely can those administering manuscript repositories work toward more adequate solutions.

Suggested Readings

Katherine E. Brand, "Developments in the Handling of Recent Manuscripts in the Library of Congress," The American Archivist, XVI (April 1953), pp. 99-104.

Verner W. Clapp, "Library Photocopying and Copyright, Recent Developments," Law Library Journal, LV (February 1962), pp. 10-15.

Henry Bartholomew Cox, "Private Letters and the Public Domain," The American Archivist, XXII (July 1965), pp. 381-388.

Herman Kahn, "World War II and Its Background: Research Materials at the Franklin D. Roosevelt Library and Policies Concerning Their Use," The American Archivist, XVII (April 1954), pp. 149-162.

Theodore R. Schellenberg, Modern Archives, Principles and Techniques. Chicago 1956, Chapter 12.

Theodore R. Schellenberg, "The Future of the Archival Profession," The American Archivist, XXII (January 1959), pp. 49-58.

Louis C. Smith, "The Copying of Literary Property in Library Collections," Law Library Journal, XLVI (August 1953), pp. 197-206.

Chapter VI

Administering the Library

A detailed statement of administrative responsibilities which would apply to every repository is impossible, but major administrative policies applicable to most manuscript libraries will be outlined in this chapter. Each library will have its own unique problems which will shape its administrative organization, but a few broad guidelines can be laid down.

Overall direction for most libraries will come from a supervisory board or committee whose authority is either implemented directly through the library staff or is part of the larger unit of of which the manuscript library is a division or branch. Sometimes these boards are chosen by the library's constituency. Again they may be appointed by a governor, mayor, college president, or similar official. Occasionally the first board of a brand new library will be selected by the original donor of the basic collection.

Although the scope and authority of these boards will vary widely, both duties and personnel frequently can be influenced by the library's chief administrator, and he has much to gain by maximizing this influence. Care in choosing or advising on personnel for the governing board and outlining its duties can pay substantial dividends. Members should be selected who best fill the needs of the library. If raising money is a primary concern, they should be chosen for the funds they can contribute or raise. If prestige is important, they should be widely known and of recognized stature in the community. If aid in acquiring manuscripts is sought, they should be acquainted with collecting and collectors. All should be thoroughly familiar with the scope and aims of the research library, sympathetically understand its function and be interested in its potential and growth.

The ideal board is one which recognizes that its primary responsibilities are to select a competent director for the library and formulate broad policy guidelines which intelligently promote its strength and growth. Board members will recognize that implementation falls within the sphere of the chief administrative officer whom they have selected, and that all other intervention in the library's internal affairs is beyond their province. There will be occasions, however, when the library should request their services for specific tasks, especially in the fund raising and collecting aspects of its work.

Selecting the chief administrator will always be the primary function of a governing board. No rules can be laid down except to say that he should be qualified. He should be competent in the subject matter field to which the library's holdings pertain, and he should have those administrative skills which will insure the selection and retention of a competent staff. He must be adept at the public relations functions which go with his office, be it publicizing a recent acquisition, or interesting a wealthy friend in making a special gift. He will have to find the wherewithal for an increase in the budget, a perennial need if the library is to grow or even to hold its own. He will have to take primary responsibility for thinking through the kind of policy decisions which will influence the use to which acquisitions can be put.

Staffing the Library

Probably more important than anything else will be the director's selection of a staff A good salary schedule will aid him immeasurably in filling this responsibility and the vigor with which he pursued an adequate budget will be a primary measure of his success. We have already talked in some detail of the specific talents needed by field representatives, catalogers, arrangers, and oral history interviewers. However there are certain broadly defined skills that can help the administrator in evaluating potential personnel. Fundamental to the usefulness of a professional staff member is a strong background in the academic discipline most pertinent to the library's holdings. The historian will find working with historical manuscripts a meaningful challenge rather than a puzzling bore. The student of American literature will be stimulated and excited by a collection of literary manuscripts. Training in the proper subject matter field will enable the staff member to empathize with the researcher. It will prove essential in the efficient preparation of finding aids, and provide the motivation for developing an acquisitions program. Some staff members will need to meet other qualifications, librarianship for example, but a scholarly background in the appropriate academic field will be an important requirement.

In most cases this will mean training in history. The historian is not only equipped to deal intelligently with the political problems which have always been his province, but is more likely than any other variety of scholar to have the skills necessary to deal with any facet of the past, be it science or literature, religion or architecture. This emphasis on training in history may lead to difficulties. The professor of history, responsible for placing graduate students, may look upon archival work as the ideal solution for misfits whom he cannot recommend for teaching positions. Some of these academic rejects have found their way into the archival profession, and occasionally they can work well in lower level jobs. More often, the same shortcomings that handicapped them as potential teachers prevent them from being successful librarians or archivists. The point is simple: beware of cast-offs from other professions.

On the other hand the trained historian can prove a problem as a staff member by letting his historical research absorb his time and interest completely. He fails to function in his archival role. He is not a librarian or archivist at all, but merely a misplaced historian. Research interest and ability are always desirable and merit encouragement. Persons with these abilities can add distinction to a library, as is demonstrated by the careers of such distinguished historian-archivists as Solon J. Buck, Randolph G. Adams, or Reuben G. Thwaites. But the time and interest devoted to research must be kept in balance with other duties or new collections will not be acquired, catalog cards will go unmade, and the needs of other investigators will not be met.

More dangerous to the reputation of a library and to the archival profession at large is the appointment of a major staff member who possesses no research or scholarly interests at all. He may be a book and manuscript dealer seeking a regular salary who convinces the library's management that he can uncover rare book or manuscript resources if he is put on the payroll. He may do just that, but it is a high price to pay for a staff member who understands little of the library's basic purpose and has no interest in its scholarly and public service functions. Again, because of the inevitable attraction of history for the aging, someone may volunteer his services to help fill his retirement years. If he possesses the necessary background, such a volunteer may contribute positively to the program. More frequently he will merely be in the way and absorb time of other staff members that could be used more productively.

If a library is big enough it will need to hire people with special technical skills such as document restoration and book binding. Ordinarily however these services are better left to outside agencies which specialize in them. A small amount of amateur restoring and repair and occasional simple binding operations can be done by an apt staff member, but the dangers of bungling should not be overlooked.

The routine operations of a manuscript library can be performed by persons with little training and experience. Much of the processing of manuscripts, such as sorting, cleaning, and arranging, falls into this category. So does the servicing of stacks. With proper supervision these tasks can be performed by unskilled workers or high school and college students. It is false economy to have highly paid professionals occupied with routine operations. Their time is too expensive to be so used and it is the quickest way to discourage a good staff member and lose him. True he may occasionally have to do a little routine or manual labor, but these should be rare occurrences indeed.

A very great asset that any new and growing manuscript library can possess for attracting and holding a competent staff is to be connected with an educational institution. Mere proximity will be a substantial help but joint appointments in subject matter fields will be the greatest boon. The level of person who can be attracted by a joint appointment in a subject matter field in a college or university and a professional position in a new manuscript library, will often be higher than that of the person who could be attracted by a library appointment alone. Whatever the formal arrangements may be, most colleges and universities informally accord the highest status and privileges to teaching faculty. Thus, if the new archive or manuscript library wants the highest type of personnel, it should seek joint appointments for its key members. In the lower echelons, graduate students (at relatively low cost) will provide a level of subject matter knowledge to which certain technical skills can be grafted. These advantages will not accrue quite so easily if the educational institution is only nearby. For example, the joint-appointment will be much more difficult, but the experience of the Minnesota and Wisconsin Historical Society libraries shows that proximity to educational institutions should not be underestimated, and their interest and cooperation is well worth wooing.

Training Programs

Formal training in archival management is offered by several institutions. In cooperation with the National Archives, the graduate school of American University initiated its first such program in 1939 under the direction of Solon J. Buck, then archivist of the United States. The program centered around a two semester graduate course in the history and administration of archives which first surveyed archival development in Europe, the British Commonwealth, and the New World, and taught the principles and techniques of archival practice in the second semester. The American University has continued its program on modern archival administration by offering an intensive one month program by well trained archivists from the faculty of the University, the National Archives and the Manuscript Division of the Library of Congress. In recent years other institutions have developed programs of their own. In 1962 Wayne State University instituted a twelve quarter hour program in archival administration and research with considerable emphasis on in-service training in the field. Also in 1962 the University of Denver began offering an institute on archival administration and regional, state and local history. This special summer course is directed by the history department of the University and the Colorado State Archives. Both Columbia University and the University of Washington now offer summer institutes.

In general this type of training program will be more useful to the budding staff member of a manuscript library than the kind of training available in many of the nation's schools of library science geared as they are almost entirely to the problems created by man's published output. But archives are not manuscript libraries, and while many problems are the same and many techniques are transferable, they cannot be accepted broadside. Participation in a good in-service training program in a well-established manuscript library, plus some exposure to archival techniques and principles either via formal courses or work experience, is, at present, the best preparation for the manuscript library staff member. Informal apprenticeship and in-service training have always supplied most of the better trained manuscript librarians, whose formal professional preparation has generally been in a subject matter field rather than in the specific techniques of manuscript librarianship.

The ultimate success of any training program will rest on its ability to attract superior trainees. Graduate students in history, with their natural predilection for studying the past and their experience with manuscripts in pursuing their own research will continue to be the richest source of staff recruitment. Whether they are ultimately committed to a career as an archivist or manuscript librarian is unimportant. Frequently they will stay, at least part-time, in the profession. If not, their training will still have given them a broader insight into the methodology of research and a keener understanding of the archivist's role. To attract good graduate students into such a program, the university itself must be of a calibre to attract their notice, for chances are that it is strength in a subject matter field rather than this specific program that originally engages their attention. After that, good relations with the pertinent academic departments and an adequately financed and staffed program will be essential. Not least important will be the need for stipends which can compete effectively with other types of graduate student support such as teaching fellowships and scholarships.

The size of the training program is limited by the size of the permanent staff. A carefully organized supervisory program will require much staff time with the trainee in its early phases. Too many students for too few staff will destroy the system. A training program is not a way to get the library's work done cheaply. While trainees will perform many tasks, they will also absorb almost as much staff time as they save. One trainee to each full-time professional staff member is a workable ratio. A larger trainee program is likely to spread staff time too thinly.

Trainees should participate actively in all phases of the library's program. Processing and the preparation of finding aids will occupy much of their time, especially in the first months of their training. Their actual contact with the kinds of materials the library is acquiring, and especially devising the means to make these materials usable to scholars, will broaden and deepen their understanding of the library's function. Servicing the library's materials as a reference assistant working directly with the library's users should be the next step in the training program. A valuable side-effect will be that the trainee's own historical horizons will be broadened by having to think about sources for a wide variety of research problems. More than one graduate student trainee has concluded that handling research requests in a good manuscript library has taught him more about approaching history's unlimited raw materials than a formal seminar. But to perform these duties satisfactorily, he will need much guidance from the permanent staff. They will not only need to teach him what answers to problems can be found in this particular library to help any given researcher on a unique problem, but also the need for tact and patience in meeting that cross-section of humanity from genealogists to distinguished scholars, which asks his assistance in the course of a year.

Trainees should meet the public in one more capacity, as participants in the collecting program. In terms of both general public relations and successful acquisitions this is the most sensitive area in which the novice will work. A blunder here can seldom be undone. For this reason experience in collecting should be left to the end of the training period, and attempted then only if his superiors have full confidence in his aptitude for this phase of the program. At no point should he be allowed to perform in this area without the active participation of a staff professional. He can accompany the field representative on calls where he is to pick up materials. He should participate in expeditions where material is being sought. He should also assist in the careful planning that precedes any work in the field, particularly when materials in a new subject matter category are being hunted down. While he will not be placed in the position of representing his institution in the field, he will have become acquainted with the general technique of collecting and the problems it presents.

The Staff Conference

In tying the various aspects of the training program together and giving it overall direction, a regular schedule of staff conferences will be invaluable. In fact, staff meetings should be held with or without a training program to ensure that all professionals are aware of and can contribute to the total operations of the library and have a proper perspective on their own niches within it. At these meetings general and specific policy decisions will be discussed. Problems involving collecting, budget, donor relations, manuscript access and restrictions are among those which will merit attention. Needless to say on many matters the administrative head of the library will make the ultimate decisions, but the collective thinking and specific knowledge of his staff will aid him. For the trainee these sessions will serve as orientation in the widest aspects of manuscript librarianship. His actual participation in the decision making process will be slight, of course, but any institution will benefit occasionally from a fresh young viewpoint. He may well be the one who asks the right question sometime.

Staff meetings should be regularly scheduled and a flexible agenda prepared. They should aim in keeping the entire staff informed of policy decisions and in sharing problems with other professionals. Occasionally outside authorities may be invited in to discuss their research interests or broaden the staff's interests.

Grantsmanship

We have already indicated that financial support, be it raising money from interested individuals, getting adequate budget appropriations from a governmental unit or larger institution of which the library is a part, or making wise decisions on the investment of an endowment, will always be basic to the successful operation of a library and one of the primary functions of its administrative officers. But at this point a specific word or two about the art of grantsmanship may be appropriate. Giving away money is one of the major 'industries' in the United States today. Some $779,000,000 was granted in 1962 by 6,007 foundations whose assets totaled 14.5 billion dollars. In addition another twenty-five million was parcelled out by 9,000 small organizations. Many more millions were handed out as gifts and bequests by individuals. The federal government dispenses enormous sums to promote research, teaching and investigation, and is now including librarbraries and collections of historical materials amongst its beneficiaries. Although science and medicine claim the lion's share of all this largesse, some money finds its way to historical societies, archives, and manuscript libraries. Cornell's regional history collection was assisted by a $25,000 Rockefeller Foundation grant in 1942. The University of Missouri received $15,000 from the same source in 1943 to start its Western Historical Manuscripts Collection. A smaller regional collection at Western Michigan University in Kalamazoo received $30,000 from a local foundation to collect materials and conduct an oral history program. A grant of a quarter of a million dollars was given to the Newberry Library of Chicago by the Carnegie Corporation for the introduction of an elaborate seminar program.

Occasionally organizations whose primary functions have nothing to do with giving away money can be interested in supporting a program in which they have a particular interest. Wayne State University's Archives has received strong financial backing for its program from a major labor union. Sometimes individual donors provide support for processing their gift or for research grants to encourage its use.

Only nationally recognized manuscript libraries have much chance of getting assistance from the major foundations. But there are many smaller foundations with regional or local interests which can be approached with much greater hope of success. The best reference work for the fund-seeker is The Foundation Directory, 2nd edition, available from the Russell Sage Foundation, 230 Park Avenue, New York, N.Y. 10017 Price: $10. Current information is dispensed by the Foundation News, 428 East Preston Street, Baltimore, Md. 21202 Price: $3 annually, a bi-monthly publication of the Foundation Library Center, 444 Madison Avenue, New York, N.Y. 10022. Although the Center does not represent any individual foundation or group of foundations nor recommend likely sources of funds, it will answer questions. A few foundations may be listed in the directories as specifically giving funds for libraries, but headings such as 'humanities' and 'arts' should also be consulted, to ensure reaching those organizations with broader interests. The approach to follow in applying for grants is simply to write a letter of request clearly outlining the proposal. There is no easy road to riches for the manuscript library, but certainly foundations are worth approaching for special projects.

Gift Evaluation

Financial gifts to libraries, museums, or educational institutions are tax deductible, a provision which stimulates giving and poses no accounting problems for the library. On the other hand the gift of manuscripts does pose problems if the donor requests an evaluation for tax purposes. Objective appraisal is difficult. Overall value may rest on such factors as the number of autographs and letters of well-known persons in a collection, its potential research value, and even such things as the research convenience of its arrangement when it arrives. Who then is to determine its worth in dollars and cents? Some libraries have members of their own staff do the evaluating. This is a questionable practice. True, the local staff person may actually be the most qualified person for the job. But to evaluate a gift to his own institution will inevitably involve him in a basic conflict. He may be tempted to overestimate to please the donor and increase his good will to the library rather than arrive at an accurate appraisal. Some institutions, such as The University Of Michigan and the Library of Congress do not permit their own staff members to evaluate materials given to them. Another solution is to refuse to take any responsibility at all for appraisal and place the full burden on the donor, but this is hardly conducive to good donor relations. The most satisfactory solution is to obtain the services of at least two outside appraisers, either professional dealers in manuscripts or professional archivists of standing and experience, preferably the former because of their greater experience in associating monetary value with materials.

Summary

Governing boards of manuscript libraries will concern themselves with broad policy decisions and the selection of a chief administrator, and should avoid involvement in the details of internal administration. Their most important task will always be the selection of a director or chief administrative officer. His success, in turn, will depend in large part on his ability to obtain adequate financial support and a competent staff.

In staffing a manuscript library training in the proper subject matter field deserves as much consideration as technical skills in library or archival work. Although formal archival training will prove more useful than most library science training programs, in-service training and experience in a good manuscript library is still the best background for a competent staff member. Staff conferences will not only play a role in such in-service training programs but are necessary to give permanent professional staff members an overview of the library's operations and a chance to contribute to policy decisions.

In meeting his financial problems the director will find that foundation support is becoming increasingly available and the possibility of obtaining such aid should be investigated especially when new programs are being inaugurated or special projects contemplated. Donors may ask an administrator to appraise their gifts for tax purposes. He should avoid involving himself and the library staff in making such appraisals by obtaining outside evaluations.

Suggested Readings

Samuel Flagg Bemis, "The Training of Archivists," The American Archivist, II (July, 1939), pp. 154-161.

Solon J. Buck, "The Training of American Archivists," The American Archivist, IV (April, 1941), pp. 84-90.

Ernst Posner, "European Experiences in Training Archivist," The American Archivist, IV (January, 1941), pp. 26-37.

Theodore R. Schellenberg, Modern Archives, Principles and Techniques. Chicago, 1956.

Ralph G. Newman, "Appraisals and 'Revenooers': Tax Problems of the Collector," American Association for State and Local History Technical Leaflet 31, History News, XX (October, 1965).

Karl L. Trever, "The Organization and Status of Archival Training in the United States," The American Archivist, XI (April, 1948), pp. 154-163.

Chapter VII

A Publications Program

Once a library has holdings, a staff, and potential researchers, the question of issuing publications will arise. Too frequently manuscript libraries have rushed into print with the first likely idea that comes to mind, rather than following a carefully thought through plan with proper attention to priorities and functions; a planned program is much to be preferred.

Functions of a Publications Program

Asking the question, 'What do we want to accomplish with our publications," is the first step in planning. A good publication program will perform four functions. First, it will give scholars information about collections, providing portable finding aids that, unlike card catalogs and inventories in manuscript form, can be used anywhere, not just in the repository itself. Guides, registers, descriptive lists and printed inventories are all devices to acquaint the potential user with a library's resources. They will save the researcher time and money both by showing him where things are and by providing reliable clues as to where they are not.

Second a good program will on occasion make primary source materials directly available to scholars or the general public by publishing the materials themselves. Third, publications can serve a training function if they are designed to pass on methodology and concepts to other archives and libraries or to assist in the transmittal of such information internally to new staff members. Fourth, publications are great spreaders of good will among donors, potential donors and users alike, and as such they serve a public relations function.

The four functions outlined above are met by different kinds of publications. However, providing information about holdings will always be a library's primary responsibility and should receive first consideration. General guides, descriptive check lists and registers or inventories to individual collections will satisfy the information-giving function.

The General Guide

The most important publication of any manuscript library is a guide to its holdings. This is the most convenient and logical way for the library to make known what it has. This means going far beyond an occasional listing of a few new accessions in a scholarly journal or news release, important though these may be. It means publication of a complete guide to manuscripts in the library.

Though the primary value and use of a guide to manuscripts may be to aid researchers who do not have access to the library's manuscript catalog, its compilation and publication will assist other phases of the library program. The best publicity a manuscript library can have is its guide. It is a graphic portrayal of your service, importance, and value to scholars, to other archivists, to administors, boards of management, donors, in fact to all those individuals and groups upon whom the library depends for its support.

If the library is well established, preparing a guide may stimulate a re-evaluation of the card catalog, perhaps leading to redoing parts of it to improve or update its style. It may bring about the recataloging of some items or collections. Such a comprehensive undertaking affords the library an opportunity to reappraise its holdings and to eliminate duplicate items or worthless materials that have somehow accumulated on the shelves.

There is no agreement on a standard format for a manuscript guide. Those published vary widely in size, shape, nature of entry, and purpose. Some are printed, hard cover publications; others may be mimeographed.

The newest and most inclusive of all guides are those which attempt to cover the entire field of manuscript collecting in the United States. A pioneering venture of this sort was Ray A. Billington, Guides to American History Manuscript Collections in Libraries of the United States (1952) reprinted from Mississippi Valley Historical Review (December, 1951) and followed in 1954 by the

Harvard Guide to American History, which includes a section on manuscripts. Neither, however, is detailed or comprehensive. More extensive is Philip Hamer's A Guide to the Archives and Manuscripts in the United States. This useful 1961 publication lists some 1,300 depositories in the United States with brief descriptions of their most important manuscript collections.

The most ambitious of all guide projects and potentially the most significant is the National Union Catalog of Manuscript Collections, three volumes of which have appeared. Long in the planning state, the project began late in 1958. The first volume published in 1962 described some 7,300 individual manuscript collections located in about 400 repositories in the United States. The second volume, published in 1964 (in two parts), listed 5,028 collections in some 350 depositories. In 1965 volume three was published covering 98 depositories and listing 2,050 collections. To describe all significant manuscript collections in public or quasi-public repositories in the United States is the objective of this monumental undertaking. Success of course depends upon the cooperation of the hundreds of depositories who must perform the most vital function of all in the Guide's preparation, providing the information about holdings for inclusion in the national catalog. However, with three volumes already published, this project is clearly established as the most important manuscript guide in print.

With publication of the National Guide, the question may be raised of why a library should publish a guide to its own holdings. In the first place, the national guide does not include all collections. The Union Catalog's requirements are too rigid and its space too limited to permit full coverage of any sizable repository's holdings. Small collections, despite their significance, cannot be listed. Lists of correspondents and subject references are also drastically limited. Second, the national catalog can be used only through its index while a depository guide can be organized topically, chronologically, or alphabetically. Third, a comprehensive guide is extremely useful for the depository itself in serving researchers both in person and by mail. Fourth, the additional cost in time and money for publishing a guide is relatively small compared with the original expense (largely in terms of staff time) required in preparing the information needed for the national catalog. The national catalog will not replace the comprehensive guide to a single library.

The steps in preparing an overall guide to a manuscript library, though requiring time and patience, are not difficult if the person performing the task knows the collection and knows history. For the new manuscript library, producing a guide can be very easy if the job is started at the time the first manuscripts arrive. The procedures and form for gathering the required data can be agreed upon and coordinated with other cataloging and finding aid procedures. Whoever catalogs the manuscripts can with little extra effort prepare the draft for a guide. Publication can be at the library's pleasure, determined by the rate of the library's growth, the size of publication it wants, and costs.

For the mature manuscript library the preparation of a guide is usually not quite so simple. In fact it may be a long drawn out procedure. Some established libraries may have perfected their cataloging techniques in their earliest days so that the catalog can be used as the basis for a guide. Most libraries will probably not be so fortunate. The catalog may have been done by many persons through the years before manuscript cataloging was well developed; thus the early catalog entries may well be inadequate. Probably the safest and surest way for an established library to proceed is to examine its records, describe them and then use the catalog as a check.

To record the necessary information the library should set up a simple form or work sheet, including places to list basic information required by the Union Manuscript Catalog and any other information the library wishes. For papers of individuals this means full name, birth and death dates, an identifying statement covering occupation, office and principal residence, as well as the nature of the materials, * their dates, their amount expressed in numbers of volumes, items or feet (to use the term "box" is not helpful unless

*Suggested designations might be: Letters (written by only the author), correspondence (letters to two or more individuals), papers (correspondence, notebooks, diaries, in effect a collection with a variety of types of manuscripts).

its size is defined) and a brief description of the contents of the collection listing all major subjects.

Preparing this description is the most difficult task in guide making. The recorder must know what topics to bring out and judge which names of correspondents should be included. The descriptive information then must be condensed into a few sentences. A distortion in proportion is inevitable. Small collections consisting of a single item or two are usually described more adequately than large collections which are more valuable. Such distortion cannot be eliminated but it can be mitigated by supplying the large collection with a more lengthy entry, including a sizable list of important correspondents. Thus the length of the description will depend on the importance of the collection and the size and scope of the eventual publication. Finally, the data sheet should include a place to note any restrictions on the collection and to list correspondents and cross references. If desired the name of the donor can be listed along with the date or dates of accessioning. *

The information gathering process need not be done in one concentrated effort. If staff size and time do not permit the assignment of a full-time professional to work on the project, it can be made a part-time or even spare-time assignment. A little can be done at a time and the task will be accomplished providing the assignment is not neglected completely. One manuscript library working in this manner completed the final project in nine years. During that time work never stopped, though it sometimes was limited to an hour or two a week. Also all current material was kept up to date so that when the existing holdings had been surveyed the new accessions were finished too.

After the information sheets have been completed and checked against the catalog, they should then be typed in the form in which they will be published. This can most effectively be done by putting them on cards which are easy to use and file, and to which additions can be made. If the information gathering process is long and drawn out, as it well might be, a system which allows additions and changes is important. An entry may have to be changed several

* See Appendix 4 for completed form.

times as new materials are placed in it or more intensive cataloging reveals new information about it.

The final draft which will go to the printer should be double spaced, full sized typewritten copy, adequately proofread and exact in form. If publication is to be by some sort of offset process, preparation of a final draft may be skipped and the information typed directly from the cards to the master sheets used in the publishing process. These master sheets are not difficult to use and are fairly easily corrected. If your library types them itself, cost can be reduced significantly. However if the time, cost and effort can be spared, a final draft is preferable because it allows an overview of the final project, simplifies the typing job, and eases the editing task.

Arranging for final publication of the completed guide is the least difficult of all the steps in the process. There are several satisfactory methods which meet nearly all needs and budget requirements. Regular printing is the most expensive means of publication. Several of the early guides of high quality took this form. Use of the offset process, which is much less expensive and yet makes a good appearance and allows a wide range of format (type size, spacing, double columns), is much more common. Lithoprinting firms are located throughout the country and there is a wide variation in their charge and in the quality of their work. It is wise to secure bids from three or four firms experienced in scholarly publication and to request samples of their publications.

Unless your collection has a heavy concentration of materials which are national in scope, the demand for the guide will probably not be large. Guides are not popular with the general public. They are reference tools and will be sought after primarily by libraries. A total distribution of 500 copies would probably be large enough for most regional collections with considerable national interest. Thus the library publishing a guide might expect to recapture publication costs but it will not make any money. If the guide is well received by scholars and makes the library's name widely known, it will have proved a success.

Registers, Inventories, and Descriptive Lists

Published registers or inventories present detailed descriptions of individual collections within the library.* A good example is the Newberry Library's 1951 inventory of the Illinois Central Railroad Collections. This 210-page document provided a detailed account of a single collection. A similar publication, though different in format, was a 1963 register of one person's papers prepared by the Syracuse University Library Manuscript Collections. This 45-page publication identified materials by box and by individual folders within a box. Archives, including those of the federal and state governments, use the inventory exclusively for publishing information about their holdings. Because of the widespread adoption of archival techniques in manuscript libraries in recent years, there has been a growing tendency toward publishing inventories and registers rather than comprehensive guides. Perhaps curators and directors have felt this trend was justified because the National Union Manuscript Catalog would serve as a substitute for the comprehensive guide to the individual repository. But this is really a false assumption, which has been discussed above. Registers and inventories will have their place in many manuscript libraries but they are no substitute for the comprehensive guide to the individual repository. They should be viewed as purely supplementary to such a guide; and where funds are limited, priority should always go to the general publication.

Descriptive lists of groups of collections will also prove a useful supplement to a general guide. Usually they will be clustered around a period or theme. A bulletin containing brief descriptive entries on Civil War diaries and letters available in one repository proved very popular during the early sixties when interest in the Civil War Centennial was at its height. The volume was useful not only to scholars of the period but its eye-catching cover and illustrations made it attractive to the general public, and it proved a great spreader of good will. Substantial gifts of similar materials resulted. Descriptive check lists of this sort could be prepared on

*Their preparation (in manuscript or published form) has been discussed in Chapter IV.

a variety of subjects, such as the westward movement, or on an important literary or political figure. Occasionally a joint effort with similar institutions could prove successful. Such a guide covering all Civil War manuscripts in a state or those pertaining to a single military engagement would be a possibility, or a guide could be made to materials scattered in several institutions that relate to a public figure.

Publication of Primary Sources

The other approach to making materials available to scholars is to publish the sources themselves. To merit this papers must be of reasonably wide interest or at least have literary merit. No one disputes the wisdom of publishing the papers of American presidents, but even here considerable selection must precede publication. The letters of a Civil War private, pioneer settler, or petty official certainly deserve much more critical scrutiny before they are deemed worthy of appearing in print. Even though any manuscript is unique in the strict sense of that word, it may so closely parallel a hundred other documents and have so little to contribute to the understanding of any broader area of concern that effort spent in editing and annotating and money used for publishing is largely wasted. The significance of the content of a series of letters or diaries, rather than the relative obscurity or fame of their author, is one crucial test. The Civil War letters of an articulate, discerning, private could have more merit and be more deserving of publication than those of an obtuse major general. But again, there may have been so many good Civil War letters and diaries published, that another is really superfluous. Meanwhile other areas of equal importance may be neglected, and general availability of similar materials should be one consideration. Not infrequently, primary sources of great literary merit deserve publication for that reason alone. Who would dispute that Mrs. Chesnut's style was as much a reason for publishing her diary as what she had to say. A recent edition of Robert Frost's letters would be another case in point.

Other Publications

"How to" publications will also have a place in a publications program, both internally where they can aid in transmitting techniques and principles to successive generations of staff, and for wider distribution by making such information available to others. Frequently publication may be too ambitious for such materials. Mimeographing or offset processes may serve the purpose nicely, and, where desirable, the items can still be copyrighted. Brochures on processing, cataloging, or collecting can all be useful, and if your techniques are good and serve well the purpose for which they are designed, it is your duty to share them with others.

Another facet of a publications program is the publishing of secondary works, usually by staff members or friends of the institution. From one point of view this is harder to justify than any other kind of publication. A repository's function is to make materials available to others for research. It can be argued that doing the research and writing is not a proper occupation of staff members who should instead be devoting their time to collecting, processing and preparing finding aids. Needless to say, the overworked staff members of most libraries are not going to do much writing. Occasionally a collection will come along which deserves a small study but which may be too parochial in scope to attract outside researchers. Also a short preliminary study on some aspect of a subject or some phase of a man's career may stimulate outside interest in the broader possibilities. Thirdly, a donor can be deeply pleased to see papers he has given used for research and the product printed, to say nothing of the benefits to a staff member's morale when he has time to work on a small study and has his organization sufficiently interested to see that it gets into print. Public relations value will be the chief reason for this kind of publication.

Last to be discussed but often first to be published by the new library is the annual report or newsletter. Here is the place to report recent acquisitions, outline future needs, describe the amount and kind of use collections are receiving and appeal for additions to budget, staff, or space. Administrators and friends, and where appropriate, legislators, need this information to keep their interest alive. Public recognition of donors in this way will serve as a partial thank you for their gifts and inspire their continued support. A more ambitious publication of this type can be used to spark a building campaign. The simple monthly or bi-monthly newsletter can be the vehicle by which a "friends" group is held together and kept interested.

Summary

The primary consideration in planning a publications program is to assure proper balance so that all four functions, information-giving, training, public relations, and publishing of original sources are met. Most important will always be providing information to the scholar and an overall guide will best meet this function. With this need met, attention can be focused on publications likely to play a larger role in facilitating good public relations and staff competence.

Suggested Readings

Philip M Hamer, ed. A Guide to the Archives and Manuscripts in the United States. New Haven, 1961.

Oscar Handlin, et al. Harvard Guide to American History. Cambridge, 1954, pp. 79-99.

Library of Congress, The National Union Catalog of Manuscript Collections. 3 vols. Ann Arbor, 1962; Hamden, Connecticut, 1964, Washington, 1965.

Fred Shelley, "The Publication Program of the Maryland Historical Society," The American Archivist, XV (October, 1952), pp. 309-320.

Murphy D. Smith, "Preparing a Manuscript Guide for a Learned Society," The American Archivist, XXV (July, 1962), pp. 323-330.

Chapter VIII

The Library and the Researcher

The primary function of the manuscript library is to serve scholarship. Its careful wooing of donors, its acquisition of a physical plant, its search for adequate processing and cataloging techniques are mere handmaidens in this task of assisting it to meet the needs of student and scholar. The proper structuring of the relationship between researcher and library involves important policy decisions. Some of the ways in which that relationship can be implemented and some of the problems to which it inevitably gives rise will be discussed in this chapter.

Orienting the Researcher - The Personal Interview

The personal interview with a staff member can be an important vehicle for insuring a smooth relationship between library and researcher. Such an interview serves to introduce the scholar or student to the facilities and practices of a particular institution and forestalls a host of later misunderstandings. It also gives at least one member of the library's staff an understanding of the researcher's needs and problems, saving him time by guiding his searches in the most fruitful direction and providing an opportunity to acquaint him with work being done by others in the same or related fields.

The interview should be conducted by any senior staff member fully acquainted with the depository's holdings and practices. It need not be the chief administrative officer. In fact, the researcher should talk with the staff member best acquainted with his own area of interest, and occasionally a short chat with more than one staff member will prove helpful. Consideration for the researcher will suggest that the interview or interviews be kept as brief as possible. No scholar struggling to draw maximum value from a limited research budget wants to have his time wasted by idle chit chat.

What should the interview cover? First of all the nature of a user's credentials should be asked for. His name, his job, the professor under whom he is working if he is a student, his research interests (unless he and his work are so well known as to require no introduction) are the minimum facts which the library has a right to know before making its resources available. How much time the researcher can spend at the repository is also essential information. The amateur buff who is interrupting a vacation trip for an hour to explore a library's resources on a Civil War battle, should expect to see the catalog for an overall view of its holdings and perhaps a typical manuscript or two, but should not be allowed to waste staff time by having two dozen collections brought to the reading room for his cursory inspection. Such situations can be avoided by a brief interview in which a visitor's credentials and the amount of time he has available have been determined.

More information will be needed from the serious scholar delving deeply into a problem on which the library has potential resources. The library must know the nature of his problem, what materials he has already used, where there are gaps in his data and how deeply and broadly he intends to dig. With this information a staff member can suggest the most fruitful areas for a scholar's searches. He may know other libraries, archives or even private individuals who have relevant materials. He will pass on the names of other scholars who are working on this or related problems. Occasionally a visitor will see this as prying. Scholars, especially immature ones, can be very wary of divulging anything about what they are finding or even what they are looking for, thus making unnecessary trouble for the library and often wasting a great deal of time for themselves. A little tact can usually solve the problem, and the reluctant informant of the first encounter usually turns chatty in a day or two and is only too eager to discuss his work and its problems.

The third task accomplished by the personal interview is the transmission of the library's rules, regulations, and restrictions on any materials he may need to use. If possible these should be in mimeographed or printed form so they can be handed to the researcher. They may consist of a formal agreement (as at the Library of Congress) to be signed by each researcher in which he agrees to abide by the rules; or individual collections may require their own rules or agreements before they can be used. (See Appendix 5 for copies of such agreements.) Then again mere knowledge of the rules may be considered sufficient and formal agreements by-passed. However rules are transmitted to the researcher, care should be taken to clarify any ambiguities, and objections should be met as reasonably and tactfully as possible.

Rules for Researchers

What are the rules that it is proper for a manuscript library to make? No one disputes the importance of insisting that materials be handled with care, that the order of collections be rigorously preserved, that only pencil, typewriter, or dictaphone be used in the taking of notes, or that the amount of material to be used by a researcher at any one time be limited. It is also clear that the library must determine what hours and days its material is to be available, and that it reserves the right, not always exercized, of inspecting brief cases and books taken from the library. Only if carrels are available will it be practical to permit the use of tape recorders. Some of these rules are for the protection of the materials themselves. Others increase staff efficiency. A third category protects other users. The size of a library and the nature of its users will determine the specific rules it will make. (See Appendix 5 for copies of rules in use in libraries.) In general the larger the number of collections and the more users a library has, the more rules it will need to make.

But in any manuscript reading room, the most obvious rules will actually have to be enforced, sometimes in the face of vigorous protest. The eminence of a scholar or the ability of a student is no guarantee that they will treat materials with care or show consideration for fellow researchers and staff. Sometimes quite the reverse is true, as ambition and self-esteem combine to produce an arrogant disregard of everyone's needs but his own. Researchers will question rules and ask that exceptions be made to them. Care should be taken in granting special privileges, for what is done for the personal friend or distinguished scholar one day, may have to be done for the amateur or casual user tomorrow, much to the eventual detriment of a library's efficiency. It is the obligation of a repository to require that a user respect its rules, regardless of whether they seem appropriate to him, suit his work habits, or fit his time schedule. Exceptions should be granted very rarely.

The Researcher and the Donor

Although it may not find expression in a formal set of rules, thought must be given to the problem of giving the researcher access to donors. While an occasional donor may be flattered by further attention from a scholar, in most cases only annoyance and worry will result. A busy person will resent requests for interviews or the filling out of lengthy questionnaires and may begin to wonder if he was wise to make the gift of materials in the first place. The elderly person or recluse who has reluctantly parted with family papers in the interests of history, finds this attempt to make personal contact almost intolerable. In general researchers should be discouraged from making direct contact with donors except where necessary to obtain permission to quote. Then it should be suggested that they make their requests by letter, keep them brief and to the point and that a personal confrontation be avoided. There will be exceptions to this rule of course. The library administrators will be in a position to judge probable donor reaction in individual cases and can advise researchers how much contact if any is likely to be wise.

Problems of Publication and Duplication

A second area of problems between user and library clusters around duplication and publication. The problem of literary rights, discussed earlier in Chapter V enters the picture at this point. Permission to publish obviously cannot be granted unless the repository possesses both literary and property rights to the material. Permission to quote for publication also assumes the library possesses these rights, and the researcher should be fully informed as to the extent of its authority and advised as to others whose literary property may be involved.

The researcher should be asked to give full credit in footnotes, preface, or bibliography for any material which he has used, whether directly quoted or not. A sample citation provided by the repository which researchers can follow will be helpful. Common courtesy suggests that the user also send a reprint of an article and advise of the publication or even send a complimentary copy of a book based on a library's holdings. A hint to this effect while a user is actually there may bring results, but it will always be difficult for an institution to keep complete records of publications based on its materials no matter how hard it tries.

Actual publication of any of a library's holdings should require the permission of a responsible administrator. Whether the quantity be large or small, the selected correspondence of a public official, a Civil War diary, or a single photograph, publication always assumes a kind of partnership on the part of the institution owning the material. The decision to permit publication is certainly a major policy matter. The request to publish single items and photographs will come most frequently, and can usually be granted. A credit line, in which the repository's name is listed accurately, should be specifically required as part of the publication permission.

Permitting publication of major holdings will pose more serious problems and may not always be in the library's best interests. Does the project interfere with publication projects of the repository itself? Usually the library's plans should be given priority, but this answer should be tempered by an objective look at the merits of the alternative scheme. Should materials be reserved for publication only under the editorship of staff members of the library or its parent institution? This has been common practice in some of the great European and American libraries, particularly when the materials were rare and additional similar papers unlikely to be available. For example, the University of Michigan's papyrus collections were purchased specifically for publication by certain scholars connected with the institution, and publication by others was restricted for several years. The Yale libraries have always given priority to their own scholars, not just in matters of publication, but in matters of use as well. Restrictions of this sort should be kept to a minimum and are harder to justify when broadened to include use as well as publication.

A more important factor in granting permission to publish should be the professional stature of the person making the request and the degree of competence he is likely to bring to the task. Scholarship will not be served by allowing a bungling amateur, unaware of standards, incapable of accuracy, dependent perhaps on his own funds and a small commercial press for the actual printing, to publish a significant manuscript. The library administrator acting as society's custodian of its materials is forced to pass on the question of the individual's competence to edit and publish in a satisfactory fashion. He has a duty to prevent poor and inadequate publication, just as he has a duty to facilitate in every way publication which is properly done. This means that he should also be cognizant of the dangers of self-interest taking precedence over scholarship. No library has a right to prevent indefinitely the publication of valuable papers by competent outsiders because at some distant day it might see fit to do the job itself.

Requests for duplication of library holdings for a scholar's own use will be an almost everyday occurrence and will bring many problems in their wake. Because of the increasing ease of getting research grants for this purpose, the pressure for duplication will continue to grow. Microfilming, Xeroxing, or photostating do enable a researcher to use papers at a time and place of his own choosing and in conjunction with related materials which may be housed elsewhere. This greatly facilitates his work and the library should make every effort to grant reasonable requests. But what is reasonable?

The answer to that question is as varied as the libraries which have materials a researcher wants duplicated. Some archives and manuscript libraries grant all requests for duplication, provided the material is open for use. Others are extremely hesitant to provide any duplicating services at all. In some cases the screening of potential researchers is itself severe, and once the request to use papers is granted, the privilege of having them duplicated follows as a matter of course. Occasionally a library has simply not thought through its policies. The answer is never simple and involves working out a series of decisions regarding relationships with donors, proper use of staff time, the necessity of preserving the integrity of collections, and its costs to the library.

Perhaps an example will illustrate the nature of the problems involved. Is it appropriate to grant the request of a Ph. D. candidate, asking by letter that all materials in a library's holdings dealing with the career of Benjamin Lundy, including letters by him and to him or other papers in which his career figures, be placed on microfilm and sent to him at his university? Is this a case in which scholarship would be served? True a thesis would be expedited, but at great cost to the library and possible disadvantage to the student. Few institutions have budgets which would justify the use of staff time for such a project. Almost always it would mean neglect of some more proper function. Libraries exist to aid the scholar and make materials available to him, but they should not attempt to do his research, and they do him no service when they try. In a case like this the library has an obligation to answer promptly and fully a query as to the nature and extent of its Lundy materials. It might eventually agree to have them duplicated for the student's use, but only after he had come to the library, examined them personally to make sure they merit further attention, and to the greatest possible extent (considering the time and funds he has available) used them at the library itself. Exceptions can be made in the case of a single item or two which might properly be Xeroxed in response to a mail request.

Even when these conditions are met there will be questions as to how far the library should go. It is a mistake to have staff time so occupied by selecting out and putting away materials for duplication that the arrangement and cataloging of new collections is neglected. The researcher should at least be required to insert flag slips for documents being removed for duplication. This alerts other users of the papers that items are temporarily missing and also facilitates refiling. The problems of refiling make duplication costs to the library far beyond the cost of the microfilming or photostating itself. The latter can be passed on to the user, but the hidden costs in staff time cannot. Also, removing materials for duplication can destroy the integrity of a collection if the ordering (or lack of it) is such that items cannot be returned to the places from which they were removed. In such cases the library will have to prohibit duplication in the interest of keeping the collection intact for future users.

What obligations should the library place on the researcher when it has agreed to duplicate materials for him? First of all, it should require that no publication be made from these copies without permission of the institution owning the originals. Secondly, it should stipulate that the researcher's films or other copies not be given to another library, at least not without permission. When microfilms of a collection are deposited in another institution open to the public, the owning library has essentially lost control of its material, thus compromising its obligations to donors and jeopardizing its controls over literary rights. With recent papers especially this can make for embarrassing and dangerous situations. For example the papers of a recent United States Supreme Court Justice contain notes about and correspondence with men who are currently sitting on the Court. Occasional items in these papers even pertain to matters germane to issues now being decided by these same justices. Needless to say indiscreet use of these papers could be very harmful to the judicial process in this country. However, their use has been carefully restricted to bona fide scholars fully cognizant of the national interest and who have been fully warned about problems of literary rights especially in connection with the authorship of letters written by persons now living. But should microfilming of these papers be permitted and these microfilms fall into other hands, as is certainly possible, all of these precautions would come to naught. The owning library would have lost control, and while it might not be legally responsible for any ensuing abuse in the use of these materials, it would be held morally responsible by the original donor and by any donors of future materials. In the long run a potential donor might destroy papers rather than make similar arrangements for their deposit, and history would be the loser.

But even in cases where literary rights and public relations are unlikely to be an issue, there are distinct disadvantages to a policy of unrestricted duplication. It prevents the library from performing one of its important services to scholarship, that of informing the researcher of others using the material or working on the problem in which he is interested.

The easiest solution to the problem of control of duplicated materials is to treat them as loans, subject to return when the scholar has finished using them. Since he then does not acquire ownership of the films, there may be some question of the propriety of charging him for their cost. Where budgets are adequate the most reasonable solution would be to do the microfilming at the library's expense and charge only a nominal rental fee. This avoids a situation where the later user of a set of films receives at no cost materials fully paid for by the first user. However, the materials filmed for most scholars will be so tailored to their individual needs that no one else will have use for them, and the person for whom they are done can quite properly expect to bear the cost.

It may seem that the preceding pages unduly emphasize the problems the researcher creates for the library and are overly protective of the library as against the scholar. Perhaps they are, but the damage that can be done by over-permissiveness in the area of duplication is great indeed, and once perpetrated it cannot be undone. As depositories acquire more and more contemporary materials, as techniques and facilities for duplication multiply, and as funds for the support of research increase, the likelihood of misuse must be consciously faced and steps taken to guard against it.

The Obligations of a Library to Its Researchers

We have examined at length the obligations of the researcher, the need for rules under which he is permitted to do his work, and restrictions which prevent him from abusing his privileges. But the library has obligations as well. They are straightforward and obvious, but they should not be overlooked.

Any manuscript library, no matter how small, must provide its users with adequate working space, decent lighting, and a reasonable schedule of hours when it will be open. Secondly, it should answer quickly and fully mail inquiries as to the nature of its resources in a specific research area. Third, it should have its holdings in usable order and equipped with adequate finding aids. The extent to which this obligation can be carried out may be limited by staff time and funds, but the responsibility should be recognized. There is no excuse for acquiring materials (especially in competition with other repositories) if they cannot be given minimal care within a reasonable time. Fourth, the library has an obligation to publicize its holdings through announcements in scholarly publications and via union catalogs, general guides, and guides to its own holdings. No manuscript library deserves to exist if it is unable to so inform scholars of its resources. Fifth, a library should be able to provide duplicating and reproduction services (where appropriate) to aid the user who cannot complete his work at the institution itself. Sixth, it should not discriminate among its users. Materials should not be withheld arbitrarily to favor certain scholars, or, something harder to control, its staff should not be allowed to play favorites in terms of promptness of service or personal help.

The manuscript staff also has an obligation scrupulously to respect the researcher's time. Service should be prompt. The user should not be interrupted every fifteen minutes with new material which he may not want and has not requested. Nor should he be subjected to idle chatter. Once the library's needs for information have been met, it should be assumed that the researcher is the best judge of how best to spend his time.

Summary

Manuscript libraries should never forget that their primary function is not the collection and preservation of written artifacts as such, but the service of scholarship. This obligation to scholarship implies broader aims than facilitating the work of any single scholar, and the larger interests of scholarship must never be sacrificed to meet the needs of a single researcher when the two are in conflict. This viewpoint should permeate all phases of a library's work. It will help shape collecting policies, play a role in decisions on processing and cataloging, but it will prove most crucial in its influence on the day to day relationships in the reading room and office with the researcher himself. It is on this principle that rules and restrictions are based. This is the guide line against which a library measures its services to the researcher.

Suggested Readings

Christopher Crittenden, "The State Archivist and the Researcher," The American Archivist, XIX (July 1956), pp. 215-221.

Robert H. Land, "Defense of Archives Against Human Foes," The American Archivist, XIX (April 1956), pp. 121-139.

John A. Munroe, "A Brave Man - Or a Foolish One," The American Archivist, XXVI (April 1963), pp. 151-160.

Howard H. Peckham, "Aiding the Scholar in Using Manuscript Collections," The American Archivist, XIX (July 1956), pp. 221-228.

Louis C. Smith, "The Copying of Literary Property in Library Collections," Law Library Journal, XLVI (August 1953), pp. 197-206.

Chapter IX

The Library and the General Public

Though manuscript libraries by design and interest are oriented toward the scholarly researcher, most are also concerned with the general public. There are few if any libraries which would limit their service and contacts exclusively to professional scholars, though they may receive primary consideration. The majority also accept a broader educational responsibility to serve the person with general interest.

The successful organization frequently requires that the public, or at least an informed segment of it, have an understanding of the library and its program. Certainly if the library depends upon the public for donation of manuscripts, the public should know about the library, the kinds of material it seeks, and what it proposes to do with them. In like manner if the library wishes to attract funds to broaden its program or finance large scale projects, construction of new quarters, for example, it is imperative for potential donors to know and appreciate the library's unique and significant role.

To get the library's message to the public for whatever reason requires imaginative planning, time, and effort. Though there is no single program for accomplishing this public relations task, all methods of disseminating information can be adapted and used to good advantage.

The appearance of staff members on the banquet circuit for school groups, service clubs, women's organizations and similar gatherings provides an opportunity to enlarge the public's knowledge of the library, to emphasize the importance of the archival profession, and to describe the library's service to society. Not that speaking tours alone will make a library famous. Only its materials and the handling of them will do that, but even directors of of well known manuscript libraries believe in the importance of these engagements in explaining their library.

A broader version of this same type of activity is the presentation of the library's role on television and radio through expository programs explaining the library, telling what it has and what it does, or through full scale dramatic renditions based on the library's holdings. For example, one effective radio series consisted of twelve fifteen-minute programs dramatizing excerpts from original manuscripts of famous persons. Weaving these excerpts into interesting narrative was done by professional radio personnel and the library staff members who were experts on the manuscripts and persons under discussion. The programs were skillfully produced with background music, careful editing, and professional dramatization. The last of the series was an informal panel discussion on colorful adventures connected with the library's manuscript collecting program. This series was taped in advance, used as a regularly scheduled part of the sponsoring university's radio programming, and then made available to local stations throughout the state and to teachers for presentation in their history classes.

Another famous library presented a series of short programs based on unusually interesting documents of national significance in its possession. These episodes were fully dramatized. In similar vein dramatized readings of a number of these documents were recorded in album form and made available to the general public. These are but examples of imaginative and tasteful ways in which the manuscript library can utilize radio and television to promote its program and to serve a useful educational function as well.

No library should overlook the value of the press release, particularly stories about interesting and significant new accessions or those with human interest. In 1964 widespread national publicity was focused on a case of manuscripts purloined from the National Archives. Though the theft and recovery of these documents can hardly be classified as the type of publicity to be sought after, it reflects interest in the manuscript library. The same interest can be used to tell the story of the arrival of an important collection of papers, unusual items in the library, or use of the materials by scholars of note. One university news service issued news releases on important anniversaries of the Civil War which contained first hand accounts found in the university's extensive files of soldiers' letters and diaries. These were widely carried by the press of the state. Similar releases can, of course, be used for all kinds of anniversary dates, celebrations, and special events.

In Chapter VII we examined the scope, usefulness, and nature of a publications program for the library. A well designed program has great value in reaching both the scholar and the general reader. Though certain publications may have to serve primarily one group or the other, there are many which can interest both. Whether the publication program means book length monographs and regularly issued periodicals or is only a mimeographed statement of the library's policies and objectives, some sort of published contact with the public will almost certainly have to be included in the library's activities.

Thus far we have examined methods of taking the library's program outside its walls. Equally important, perhaps more so, is a program designed to get people into the library both for public relations value and education as well.

For regular and active backing some libraries establish supporting boards or societies, which are labeled "Friends of the Library," "Board of Honorary Curators," or similarly entitled. If its constituency is large enough, the library may have two or three or more of these boards, committees, or supporting organizations with varying functions to fit special needs and requirements.

If these are to be active boards, the members should be interested in the library or be persons whom the library wishes to interest. In the latter category there is a temptation sometimes to select members for the prestige their names will lend. To be sure, there is merit in such an approach, but if a prestigious person has no real interest in the library or commitment to it, he will remain only a figurehead and add little.

Supporting societies or boards can perform many useful

functions. For most libraries the paramount one is bolstering the budget. This responsibility may involve a long term program of great scope such as securing funds for a building or establishing an endowment; or it may be more limited, such as raising money for equipment or manuscript purchase. Raising large amounts of money for major projects such as building construction involves elaborate campaigns and usually professional advice from fund raising agencies. For smaller sums, however, the friends of the library (or its own staff) can attract gifts from organizations or people having a particular interest in historical agencies. Patriotic societies are likely prospects for financing document acquisition or repair, publications, or special research projects. Donors of materials by their very action in depositing their papers have indicated interest in the library and may be induced to support it financially as well. University-connected libraries can seek out alumni. All of these groups if tactfully approached and shown the need for their benevolences can contribut significantly to the manuscript library's program. Fund raising carried on indirectly through the boards is often more effective than that conducted by the library staff itself.

Supporting societies or boards can effectively promote the library's program in other ways as well. If the library collects by gift, board members can suggest persons to contact for materials and arrange interviews with prospective donors. They can assist in publicizing the program and effectively "lobby" for the library in the state legislature, city council, university board of trustees, or wherever the library receives its main support.

But they can have a potential negative influence. A board member may use his position to promote his own prestige, to secure special privileges for himself, or even to serve his own private collecting interests. Not so drastic as any of these but more common is meddlesomeness, which though it may do little harm will cause extra work and wasted time. Board members may push their own special historical interests onto the library, negating or at least spoiling the impact and symmetry of a carefully arranged collecting theme. They may try to influence staff selection. Or at the very least they may cause the director to lose many hours of time just listening to them and keeping them contented. Thus though the supporting society or advisory board can do much good, care must be exercised in filling its membership or it will be at best a neutral factor or a meddlesome group that is only an obstacle for the library.

Although most libraries welcome the general public's financial support and approbation, some discourage use of their materials by all except professional scholars or advanced graduate students. One famous library required an elaborate academic pedigree before permitting use of its materials, but even this library encouraged the general public to enter its magnificent main hall to view the exhibits.

Even when there is no imposing room available for display purposes, the library's manuscripts, pictures, posters, and other materials can be arranged in modest surroundings that will be appropriate, interesting, and significant. The exhibits should emulate the practice of the modern museums by telling a story or illustrating a theme relating to the library's program. A miscellaneous assortment of unrelated documents even of great rarity and importance will serve no good purpose. All items used should be either self-explanatory or carefully described in brief, easy to read labels. It will only annoy your patrons to display an unlabeled letter which is difficult to read. In fact, cases filled only with letters, diaries, unrelieved by pictures, maps, or other visually appealing materials will have little impact on the general public, no matter how interesting they may be.

It will do no good, of course, to work out an exhibit with care and imagination and then have no one see it except the usual researchers. This can happen unless the library show cases are located where the public or a significant section of it passes by or unless steps are taken to attract attention. To bring people to the exhibit it can be publicized generally through the news and information media. Particularly effective are personal invitations and distribution of descriptive programs of the exhibit.

Such invitations may announce a formal opening for the exhibit, including refreshments and a program. Whether or not social activities are used in conjunction with an exhibit, they and the program are useful in bringing the public into the library. Everyone enjoys a party so there is no reason why parties cannot be used effectively by a historical library. They can be annual affairs commemorating historical events or occasions in the library's past. They may be held to honor donors or friends of the library, or for that matter, for no reason at all.

Tours of the library arranged for special groups afford a good opportunity to explain its operation and portray its function. These activities take time and therefore must be arranged so as not to impose too great a strain on the staff. Nor should they be conducted if they are a great annoyance to regular researchers. With these conditions met, the tour can be arranged to fit the interests of the group. The processing of manuscripts can be explained; interesting manuscripts can be shown; and explaining the use to which materials are put affords an excellent opportunity to educate the public about the library. If skillfully done there is probably no better way to make clear what the library is all about.

Some libraries arrange regular programs organized around their holdings. A labor archives, for example, might sponsor a series of talks by early labor leaders which could serve a useful educational function for both the scholarly and non-scholarly public, focus attention on the library's program, and stimulate donations of important collections. Any number of programs can be worked out around all kinds of themes to meet the library's requirements and to interest patrons.

The single program or the program series can be expanded to a series of seminars or a conference. Interest in history, particularly local, regional, or state history, has never been greater than it is today. A conference with a lively program can be potentially most useful. Many state historical societies with or without manuscript collections have long employed the annual meeting or history conference to sustain interest in their work. There is no reason why a manuscript library either by itself or in conjunction with other historically interested groups can't do the same.

The program can center in part or altogether around the library itself, what it is doing, how it is doing it, and methods of research for the amateur researcher. Or subject matter areas represented in the library's manuscript and printed materials can serve as the focal point for programs of value both to the general public and the professional scholar. These programs can be regularly scheduled events or occasional soirees, their content as widely varied as the library's time, talent, and purpose will allow.

We have already discussed the library's responsibilities and techniques in dealing with the scholarly researcher. On a different plane there is the problem of handling the amateur researcher who wishes to use the library's books and manuscripts. Much of what applies to the scholar also applies to the non-professional researcher. Adequate quarters and finding aids and guides should be available to him. He too should have a personal interview which, in fact, might be of more value to him and save more time for the library than in the case of the professional. The interview permits identification of the researcher who seeks only gossip in collections of important people or has other improper motives for his work so that his use of materials can be restricted. The extensiveness of the contemplated research project can be ascertained. Most amateurs have simple projects that can be easily fulfilled with a limited amount of materials. There is danger in confusing the amateur by giving him too much material or material which he has no skills to use properly. For example, to give a casual researcher interested in his home town, church records, correspondence files of persons who lived in the community, and other manuscript records would probably bewilder him rather than help him. A county history or two perhaps supplemented with some local newspapers would no doubt answer his needs better and save staff time as well.

The amateur researcher usually needs to become acquainted with the finding aids and general research resources available. Many will never have used a manuscript guide or catalog, and though for some there will be no need to use manuscript material, there are those who wish to and need to. They will have to be informed of the indexes, guides and catalogs that are available, and of course briefed on the rules for use of manuscripts. Although many libraries discourage or even prohibit amateur use of manuscripts and rare books, the amateur is more likely to be careful and conscientious about document use than the professional. He is frequently a bit awed and moreover is not likely to compare your rules and service with a dozen other manuscript libraries already visited. Be prepared when dealing with the amateur for loquaciousness. Not limited by time or deadlines like the professional scholar, he is inclined to visit. Furthermore, if he has never used manuscripts before, he may become enthralled with his findings and wish to share them with you and all the researchers who come within listening distance. Firm but kindly reminders of the necessity for undisturbed quiet are in order.

The most common type of amateur researcher is the genealogist. The availability of published or unpublished genealogies, census records, and church records will invariably attract genealogical research. The library will have to decide if it will include materials specifically useful to genealogists or discourage them from coming to the library. These researchers are often viewed as pests because they take valuable staff time without adding much to history. Consequently many manuscript libraries including some of the most important discourage them. On the other hand, the genealogist can be of considerable assistance. One manuscript library, for example, found that an influential pressure group in its drive to win approval for a new building was the local genealogical society, which contained representatives of some of the town's leading families. Genealogists too can be helpful in securing manuscript collections. With interest in the library aroused by their genealogical research, these persons can obtain leads on important collections. Also true is the fact that with the expanded use of social science methods, genealogical materials have become useful to serious scholars in history, sociology, political science, and other social sciences. Studies of various political and professional groups, for example, may rely heavily on a mass of biographical and genealogical data. No library wants to become merely a center for gerontological therapy with crowds of old folks looking up their ancestors (a plan which was actually seriously suggested to one library), but it must at least give some thought to what its role should be in dealing with a group which is bound to come around.

A further problem brought on by the genealogical researcher, and others as well, is to what extent should research requests by mail be answered. All libraries have the responsibility at least to tell the inquirer if they have materials of use to him, although some libraries do not even do this. Beyond that, the service rendered will depend on the amount of staff time available. One eastern library set an arbitrary limit of twenty minutes on each mail request. Others suggest persons in the locality skilled in this type of research who will do the researching for a fee. Whatever the solution chosen, the library can rest assured that the problem will occur and grow as the library grows.

Summary

For most manuscript libraries it is vital or at least highly desirable to have their program as widely known to the general public as possible. By speaking appearances, radio and television programs, and newspaper stories the library can carry its story out to the public or can bring the public to its doors by organizing supporting societies and boards, arranging interesting programs, conferences and social affairs and by attractive exhibits.

The library will also have to serve the general public which wishes to use its materials. These amateur researchers should be informed of the library's rules on the use of manuscripts and assisted in using its finding aids by interviews with a staff member. Such a meeting will save both researcher and staff time. Genealogists, if permitted, will probably form the most common type of non-professional researcher. They can use up much staff time but also may assist the library in obtaining manuscripts, winning support, and stimulating financial gifts.

Suggested Reading

Lucile M. Kane, "The Exhibition of Manuscripts at the Minnesota Historical Society," The American Archivist, XV (January, 1952), pp. 39-45.

William D. McCain, "The Public Relations of Archival Depositories," The American Archivist, III (October, 1940), pp. 235-244.

Kenneth W. Richards, "The State Archivist and the Amateur Researcher," The American Archivist, XXVI (July, 1963), pp. 323-326.

Appendix I

Location Guide

A. Personal Papers

Shelved alphabetically under name of collection. "Guide to Manuscript Collections in Michigan, Vol. I, Michigan Historical Collections, University of Michigan," useful catalogue up to September, 1941, holdings of Michigan Historical Collections; for cataloging of material transferred from the Rare Book Room of the University Library see "Guide to Manuscript Collections in University of Michigan, Vol. II, University of Michigan Collections."

[A symbol followed by capital letter indicates bound volume.
A symbol followed by lower case indicates unbound material.]

Classified in five divisions according to physical type:

AA Bound manuscripts (e.g., diaries, letterpress books, scrapbooks, personal account books, etc.) Room 160.

Portfolios of manuscripts and seminar papers. Upright on shelves, Room 160.

Aa Unbound papers, collections of personal papers, unbound, miscellaneous personal papers. Filed horizontally in black manuscript boxes, steel shelves, Room 156.

Ab Upright boxes of personal papers for large or especially valuable collections. Room 168.

AC Bound manuscripts, outsize, steel shelves. Room 156.

Ac Unbound manuscripts, outsize. Filed in outsize manuscript boxes, horizontal. Room 156.

B. Archives of Organizations, Agencies and Institutions.

Bound volumes, Rooms 160 and 164; unbound materials, Room 166, except as especially noted. Bound volumes, outsize, steel shelves, Room 156. Unbound volumes, outsize, outsize manuscript boxes, horizontal, Room 156.

[B symbol followed by capital letter indicates bound volume.
B symbol followed by lower case indicates unbound material.]

BA Religious organizations, arranged in alphabetical order by official name of organization or, in the case of churches, denomination. Subdivisions of each denomination from largest to smallest. Smallest subdivision, namely, local churches within each denomination, filed alphabetically by town. Bound volumes, Room 160.

BA Outsize. Room 156.

Ba Religious organizations. Unbound materials, arranged as in BA, filed in horizontal manuscript boxes, Room 166.

Ba Outsize. Room 156.

BB Business records of individual firms. Bound volumes, Room 164.
1. Nationally known firms, alphabetically, by firm.
2. Local firms, by town, and alphabetically by firm within each town.

Bb Business records of individual firms. Unbound materials, except as specially noted, Room 166.

BC Business organizations and leagues (bankers' associations, Business and Professional Women's Club, etc.) Bound volumes, Room 160.

Bc Business organizations and leagues. Unbound materials, Room 166.

BD Fraternal, racial, national origin groups. Alphabetically arranged under official title of organization. (Does not include University fraternities and sororities, which are filed under BImuF47). Bound volumes, Room 166.

Bd Fraternal, racial, national groups. Unbound materials, black manuscript boxes, Room 166.

BE War-born Groups. Bound volumes, Room 160.
1. Patriotic groups. (D. A. R., S. A. R., etc.)
2. Veterans' groups. (V. F. W., American Legion, etc.)
3. Military groups, local (Brady Guards, Nat'l Guards, etc.)
4. War relief agencies.

Be War-born groups. Unbound materials, black manuscript boxes, Room 166.

BF Medical and health groups. Bound volumes, Room 166.
1. Medical journals (manuscript correspondence)
2. Medical associations,
3. Hospitals, hospital associations and publications.

4. Health associations.

Bf Medical and health groups. Unbound materials, Room 166.

BG Agricultural groups and organizations. Bound volumes, Room 160.

Bg Agricultural groups and organizations. Unbound materials, Room 166.

BH Educational organizations (M. E. A., P. T.A., etc.) Bound volumes, Room 160.

Bh Educational organizations. Unbound materials, Room 166.

BI Educational institutions - private schools, colleges (public schools under CC, cities and communities). Alphabetically arranged by name of institution. (BImu University of Michigan location catalogue found in Appendix A, pp. I) Bound volumes, Room 166.

Bi Educational institutions. Unbound materials, Room 166.

BJ Social reform groups and organizations. (general social reform, temperance, anti-slavery, suffrage, etc.) Bound volumes, Room 166.

Bj Social reform groups and organizations. Unbound materials, Room 166.

BK Men's and Women's clubs, social. Bound volumes, Room 166.
- .M Men's Clubs.
- .W Women's Clubs.

Bk Men's and Women's Clubs, social. Unbound materials, Room 166.

BL Governmental clubs. (e.g. House and Senate Club) Bound volumes, Room 166.

Bl Governmental clubs. Unbound materials, Room 166.

BM Civic groups and organizations. Bound volumes, Room 166. (Rotary Club, Chamber of Commerce, etc.) and Foundations.

Bm Civic groups and organizations. Unbound materials, Room 166, and Foundations.

BN Scientific organizations. Bound volumes, Room 166.
1. Professional, alphabetically by profession.
2. Amateur, alphabetically, by nature. (Garden Clubs)

Bn Scientific organizations. Unbound materials, Room 166.

BO Legal organizations. Bound volumes, Room 166.

Bo Legal organizations. Unbound materials, Room 166.

BP Cultural organizations. Bound volumes, Room 166.
1. Art
2. Drama
3. Historical
4. Literary
5. Musical

Bp Cultural organizations. Unbound materials, Room 166
1. Art
2. Drama
3. Historical
4. Literary
5. Musical

BQ Labor groups, by Unions. Bound volumes, Room 166.

Bq Labor groups, by Unions. Unbound materials, Room 166.

BR Recreation and sport groups. Bound volumes, Room 166.
1. Statewide
2. Upper Peninsula
3. Lower Peninsula
4. Local, alphabetically by town or community
5. Individual recreational clubs of more than local interest.

Br Recreation and sport groups. Unbound materials, Room 166.

BS Foundations (Ford; Kellogg; Kresge, etc.)

BT Political groups and parties. Bound volumes, Room 166. [See FT for subdivisions of BT]

Bt Political groups and parties. Unbound materials, Room 166.
(See FT for subdivisions of BT]

BU Press Clubs. Bound volumes, Room 166.

Bu Press Clubs. Unbound materials, Room 166.

BZ Library groups and associations. Bound volumes, Room 166.

Bz Library groups and associations. Unbound materials, Room 166.

C. General Michigan History, Governmental Organizations, and Descriptions.

Bound material in Room 166; unbound materials in Room 166; outsize bound volumes on steel shelves, Room 156; outsize unbound materials in outsize manuscript boxes, Room 156.

[C symbol followed by capital letter indicates bound volume. C symbol followed by lower case indicates unbound material.]

CA State as a Unit
Michigan relations with the Federal Government
Michigan relations with Canada
Michigan relations with other states

1. Constitution of the state of Michigan, constitutional conventions and amendments.
2. Judicial affairs
   a Territorial
   b State
   c Federal
3. Legislative affairs
   a Handbooks
   b Journals
   c Bills
   d Laws
4. Organization of government
   a Governor
   b Officials, boards, commissions, etc. (See Appendix B)
   c Federal agencies and departments in Michigan.
5. General history and description, including travels in Michigan.
   a General Michigan history, by author
   b Period history, chronologically
      French regime to 1760.
      British regime, 1760-1796.
      Northwest Territory, 1796-1805.
      Michigan Territory, 1805-1836.
      Indian treaties, by date.
      Mexican War
      Civil War.
      War of 1898 (Spanish-American).
      World War I.
      World War II.
   c Subject history, alphabetically by subject.
      (See Appendix C for list of subjects. Pp XVI)

d Great Lakes. History and description.
6. Lower Peninsula. Histories and description, general
   a Southeastern Tourist Association and lesser general units within the area.
   b Western Tourist Association and lesser general units within the area.
   c Eastern Tourist Association and lesser general units within the area.
7. Upper Peninsula. Histories and description, general units within the area.
8. The teaching and the writing of Michigan history.
9. Michigan anniversaries and celebrations, including Michigan exhibits at fairs.

CB Counties. Collective township and county materials go at beginning of section.
1. Counties, alphabetically.
2. Townships, alphabetically under county.

CC Towns, cities, localities, lakes, islands, etc.
1. [Directories]
2. General history
3. Specific history
4. Description
5. Government (governmental boards and agencies)
6. Educational and cultural institutions
7. Special events

Picture Locations

U. Pictures. "U" symbol indicates pictures. In general, the classification followed for pictures is that of manuscript, both in the University section and in the non-University section. In steel file and picture drawers, Room 160 (Some in 164)

UA Individuals, alphabetically by name, including family groups and family residences.
UAs means small-sized picture
UAm means medium-sized picture-applying to all pictures.
UAl means large picture - Room 156

UB Organizations and organized groups, including views of buildings used exclusively as headquarters. (All identifiable individuals cross-referenced by name in catalog.)

BA Religious groups.
Arranged in alphabetical order by denomination. Subdivisions of each denomination, according to size, from state and sectional divisions to local churches.

BB Business firms.
1. Nationally known, by name alphabetically
2. Small or local, by town, and alphabetically within each town.

BC Business organizations and leagues.
Includes Business and Professional women's clubs

BD Fraternal and racial associations and groups. Alphabetically arranged under name of fraternity or organization. (University fraternities, UBImuF47)

BE War-born groups.
1. Patriotic groups (D. A. R., S. A. R.)
2. Veterans' groups (V. F. W. American Legion, etc.)
3. Military groups, local (Brady Guards, Nat'l Guard, etc.)
4. War relief agencies

BF Medical and health groups.
1. Medical associations
2. Hospital associations
3. Health associations

BG Agricultural associations.

BH Educational organizations (N. E. A., P. T. A.)

BI Educational institutions - private schools, colleges.

Appendix II

Inventory

Henry Howland Crapo Papers

General description of correspondence

1843-1855	Most of the correspondence is with various agents and others about land purchases and holdings in Ohio, Michigan, Iowa, etc. The Michigan men with whom he corresponded during this period include Harvey Williams, William Mercer, Isaac Christiancy, Daniel Bacon, Henry Ledyard, Orrin Baker, William Driggs and William Fenton.
1855-1865	Most of the correspondence with H.H. Crapo's son, William W. Crapo, about the father's personal business and political affairs, and includes material in rich detail on his lumbering, railroad and political activities.
1866-1869	Much of the correspondence is with W.W. Crapo and with H.H.C. Smith, Crapo's son-in-law and business associate. In '68 and '69 many of the letters deal with Crapo's illness, but there is still considerable material on business and political affairs, especially the Senatorial campaign of 1868, the railroad act vetoes, and various messages to the Legislature.
1870's	This correspondence is between W.W. Crapo and H.H.C. Smith and others managing the Michigan end of the Crapo estate.
1878-1895	Correspondence of W.W. Crapo with various agents, including H.C. Platt and Orrin Potter about the Crapo land holdings in various states, principally those which were part of the Eber Ward estate. 1888-1890 there is more general correspondence of W.W. Crapo including some matters pertaining to his activities in Congress during that period.
1896-1920	Most of the correspondence is that of Stanley T. Crapo, som of W.W. Crapo about the Crapo farm near Flint.

Shelf List

Henry Howland Crapo Papers

Box 1 - Correspondence 1830 - Dec. 1852
Box 2 - Correspondence Jan.-Dec. 1853 and indices to letters received, August 1853-1856
Box 3 - Correspondence Oct. 1853-May 1854
Box 4 - Correspondence June 1854-March 1855
Box 5 - Correspondence April 1855-December 1855
Box 6 - Correspondence January 1856-June 1857
Box 7 - Correspondence July 1857-September 1859
Box 8 - Correspondence October 1859-March 1862
Box 9 - Correspondence April 1862-June 1864
Box 10 - Correspondence July 1864-September 1866
Box 11 - Correspondence October 1866-April 1868
Box 12 - Correspondence May 1868-August 1869
Box 13 - Correspondence September 1869 -1879
Box 14 - Correspondence 1880-1887
Box 15 - Correspondence 1888-June 1896
Box 16 - Correspondence July 1896-1920
Box 17 - J.C.Willson's synopsis and daily notes on the care of H.H. Crapo
Record of his last illness kept by H.H. Crapo
Resolutions on death of Crapo
Last will and testament of H.H. Crapo
Obituaries of Crapo
Biographical notes on Crapo made by his son, W.W. Crapo
Clipping file assembled by Crapo, 1852, 1859, 1860-1869 and undated
Pictures of Crapo and Crapo family
Box 18 - Notes for political campaigns, 1861-1863
Notes on various subjects pertinent to his term in the State Senate
Notes on agriculture and general conditions in Michigan assembled by him as background for the governorship
List of pardons made by Crapo, 1865-1866
Papers and clippings dealing with his railroad bill vetoes
Campaign papers, 1866
Report, Dec. 31, 1866, of the Adjutant General of the U.S. on the status of the Michigan militia
Notes and papers on the negro suffrage amendment
Notes for [Thanksgiving ?] proclamation
Box 19 - Speeches and addresses and articles by H.H. Crapo and notes for same
Box 20 - Miscellaneous papers, 1827-1866 and undated
National Loan Fund Life Insurance Society papers, 1847-1850
Papers relating to first Michigan land purchase, 1835
Papers relating to Ohio lands, 1847-1890
Personal and business cards, 1858-59

Box 21 - Papers relating to the purchase of the Driggs tract
Papers relating to H.H. Crapo's settlement with James Arnold, his original partner, in December 1859
Sash factory account, 1867-68
Flint yard stock account, 1868

Box 22 - Descriptions and maps - Michigan lands
Miscellaneous pine lands papers, 1850-1869
Journal of W.W. Crapo lands, 1878-1884
Miscellaneous maps and broadsides relating to pine lands

Box 23 - Papers relating to the Ward lands, 1873-1902, including copy of the will of Eber Ward

Box 24 - Notebooks dealing with E. B. Ward lands, Ottawa and Lucas County lands, and miscellaneous Michigan lands; scale of logs sawed 1869; printed materials on Flint and Pere Marquette Railroad, including traffic reports, 1893, promotional materials and typescript of Flint and Pere Marquette exchange of facilities with Pennsylvania Railroad

Box 25 - Miscellaneous notebooks and printed materials dealing with agricultural activities of Henry and W.W. Crapo, principally the breeding of Hereford cattle
Political manual for 1866
Bible of Henry Crapo
General Railroad law, 1859
Story of the cotton industry in New Bedford, Mass. by Crapo's grandson, H.H. Crapo

Box 26 - Receipts and vouchers, 1820-1836
Box 27 - Receipts and vouchers, 1837-1841
Box 28 - Receipts and vouchers, 1842-1844
Box 29 - Receipts and vouchers, 1844-1847
Box 30 - Receipts and vouchers, 1840's
Box 31 - Receipts and vouchers, 1848-1852
Box 32 - Receipts and vouchers, 1852-1894 and undated
Address of W.W. Crapo, 1919, referring to Henry H. Crapo
List of items removed from Crapo papers

Boxes 33 to 35
Land records, deeds, tax deeds, etc.

Shelf List

Henry Howland Crapo bound manuscripts

Shelf I

Executive Journal of State of Michigan, 1865-1867	2 v.
Journals and diaries of Henry H. Crapo, 1854-1864	8 v.
Journals of Henry H. Crapo, 1868-1869	2 v.
Journals, 1874-75, 1877-79, of W.W. Crapo and others, mostly pertaining to the Crapo farm	5 v.

Ms. of an address by Henry H. Crapo to Genesee County Agric. Soc.	1 v.
Scrapbook, 1866-1869, on second gubernatorial term	1 v.
State Military Agency, soldiers' relief fund, 1865	1 v.
Political notebooks, 1864 and 1868, stating plan of campaign for election of 1864 and Senatorial election of 1868	2 v.

Shelf II

Swamp lands notebook, 1865, re road building contracts, etc.	1 v.
Memorandum and account books, 1841-1851, for various Massachusetts properties of Henry H. Crapo	14 v.
Farm journals and ledgers, 1888-1902, for Crapo farm	14 v.
Stock breeding record books	2 v.
Letter press books, 1853-1857, of Henry H. Crapo	6 v.

1 box of small notebooks and diaries including:
- Lake Superior Memorandum, July 11, 1865
- personal account book, 1844-45
- diaries, 1854 and 1867
- Memorandum books, 1854-55, 1856, 1857-58, 1860, 1863-64, dealing chiefly with lumbering activities
- Journal, 1853, of a trip to the Michigan pine lands

Inventory
Alexander G. Ruthven Papers
(1929-1951)

The Ruthven papers for the period 1929-1951 are really the papers of the President's Office of The University of Michigan. As such they form the single most comprehensive source of information on the affairs of the University for that period, and are only very partially and incidentally Ruthven's personal papers. They contain no correspondence that does not pertain to his professional life and no personal financial records. For this reason they have been kept as an independent unit, not incorporating into them the scattered materials in the Michigan Historical Collections covering other periods of his career.

The papers have been left in original order in the filing system inaugurated and maintained by Ruthven's secretary, Ruth Rouse. Miss Rouse filed all outgoing and incoming correspondence and other papers in a single alphabet by academic year. The only exception to this was Invitation Regrets and accepts for Ruthven himself and the University as a corporate body which were filed in a separate alphabet by city or town or occasionally by the group offering the invitation. The main file is largely a correspondent file and papers relating to most of the University's schools and departments are also filed under the name of the dean or department chief. However, there are exceptions to this rule, i. e., Clements Library, football, fraternities, Board in Control of Intercollegiate Athletics, Lawyer's Club, Naval ROTC, ROTC, Senate Advisory Committee, Board in Control of Student Publications, Student Religious Association, and Radio and Television studios in the last years of his administration. However, it is usually safe to look first under the name of a faculty member or staff officer for matters falling within his jurisdiction or control. Other matters which are filed under subjects rather than under persons are: acknowledgments; applications; correspondence with associations, bureaus, etc.; fellowships, scholarships and loans; foreign institution aid; foreign students; membership; questionnaires; U. S. legislative matters (filed variously under U. S. Legislation and Legislation U. S.); U. S. departments;

and visitors.

In addition to papers dealing with University of Michigan affairs there are full files on related organizations and professional activities: i. e., the American Council on Education, American Philosophical Society, Association of American Universities; Economic Club of Detroit; Conference of Governing Boards of the Council of State College Presidents; and the Institute of International Education.

The catalogue cards give both the date of correspondence and the name of the file. The date will tell you which academic year a letter falls within; the name of the person who wrote the letter will indicate its place in the alphabet unless it is to be found in some other file. In this case the name of the correct file is indicated in parentheses after the date. For example the card catalogue under Hull, Cordell, states that there is a letter, November 30, 1940 (Latin America file) from Hull in the Ruthven papers. This means that in the papers for July 1, 1940-June 30, 1941 such a letter will be found filed under Latin America.

No attempt was made to catalogue material on University departments, staff members, and policies unless a comprehensive statement had been prepared at some particular time, summarizing problems and policies or pointing toward future solutions and plans. It was assumed that any researcher interested in the University or its staff would automatically go to the Ruthven papers. Catalog cards have been prepared only for those faculty members with whom there was considerable correspondence.

The cross-reference list which follows the shelf list will give the researcher some idea of the scope of the papers and the range of the list of Ruthven's correspondents.

Box	General File	Box	General File
1	1929-30	6	1933-34 (A-O)
2	1930-31	7	1933-34 (P-Z)
3	1931-32 (A-N)		1934-35 (A-F)
4	1931-32 (O-Z)	8	1934-35 (G-Z)
5	1932-33 (F-Z)	9	1935-36 (A-O)

Box		Box	
10	1935-36 (P-Z)	13	1937-38 (O-Z)
	1936-37 (A-F)		1938-39 (A-B)
11	1936-37 (G-Z)	14	1938-39 (C-R)
12	1937-38 (A-N)		

. . . and so forth

Cross Reference List For Ruthven Papers:

Acheson, Dean Gooderham
Adams, Henry Carter
Adams, James Pickwell
Adams, Randolph Greenfield
Ala, Hussein
Allen, John
American Council on Education
Ames, Joseph S
Angell, Carleton Watson
Angell, James Rowland
Angell, Robert Cooley
Ann Arbor, Mich. City Council
Ann Arbor School of Religion
Athletics
Babst, Earl D
Baits, Vera Burridge
Baker, Newton Diehl
Baker, Ray Stannard
Ball, Joseph Hurst
Barbour, Thomas
Barger, George
Bartlett, Harley Harris
Bates, Henry Moore
Beal, Junius Emery
Bentley, Alvin Morell
Bevis, Howard Landis
Billington, Ray Allen
Bingay, Malcolm Wallace
Bishop, William Warner
Bizzell, William Bennett
Bliven, Bruce
Bonner, Campbell
Booth, Evangeline Cory
Boring, Edward Garrigues
Bradley, Omar Nelson
Bricker, John William
Brooks, Van Wyck
Brown, Joe Evan
Brown, Prentiss Marsh
Brown, William E
Brucker, Wilber Marion
Brumm, John Lewis

Appendix III

Diary Inventory

1. Name ____________________
   Birth and death dates ____________________
2. Place of birth ____________________
   Residence in America ____________________
3. Occupation ____________________
   ____
4. Time span of diary ____________________
5. Contents ____________________
   ____
   ____
   Main interests of diarist ____________________
   ____
   ____
   Significant events in the American scene ____________________
   ____
   Notes on spelling and diction ____________________
   ____
   Style (whether readable, interesting, dull, etc.) ____________________
   ____
6. Location of diary Michigan Historical Collections.
7. Page length ____________________
   Number of pages ____________________

S C R A P B O O K Inventory

1. NAME OF COLLECTOR ____________________

   BIRTH & DEATH DATES ____________________

2. PLACE OF BIRTH ____________________

   RESIDENCE IN AMERICA ____________________

3. OCCUPATION ____________________

4. TIME SPAN ____________________

5. MATERIAL IN SCRAPBOOK (Printed, manuscript, & General Types) ____________________

6. CONTENTS:

   (a) Principal Subjects ____________________

   ____

   (b) Places ____________________

   ____

   (c) Organizations ____________________

   ____

   (d) U of M events ____________________

   ____

   (e) Special events ____________________

   ____

   (f) Other ____________________

   ____

7. LOCATION Michigan Historical Collections

8. PAGE LENGTH ____________________

9. NUMBER OF PAGES ____________________

Appendix IV

Information Form
Michigan Historical Collections
For Guide to the Manuscript Collections, Second Edition

Names and dates: Moody, Arthur Blair 1902-1954

Paper, dates: Papers, 1930-1954

Number or footage: 30 feet and 38 volumes

Occupations and information: Detroit News Washington correspondent; U.S. Senator. Extensive files of personal correspondence, including letters from Moody to his wife, Mother and other members of his family; but chiefly correspondence files dealing with his professional career as both a newspaperman and a Senator; correspondence with editors, readers, informants and colleagues. There are manuscript addresses, notes, newspaper articles, tapes of radio programs; appointment books while U.S. Senator; three volumes containing his voting record in the Senate; 34 volumes of scrapbooks of newspaper articles he wrote; films.

See Guide, first edition, for additional information ____ yes x no

Restrictions: None

Gift of Mrs. Blair Moody (date) 1956 or

Purchased (date)________

Correspondents include:

Bernard M. Baruch
William Benton
Chester Bowles
Paul Hoffman
Harry L. Hopkins
Estes Kefauver
John F. Kennedy
William F. Knowland
John J. Sparkman
Harry S. Truman
G. Mennen Williams
Charles E. Wilson

Cross References:

Democratic Party
Election of 1952
Journalism
New Deal
Politics
U.S. Senate
World War, 1939-1945

Appendix V

Archives Handling of Oral History Transcripts

1. Transcripts will be available to the following classes of persons:

    a. regular academic faculty at a recognized college or university engaging in objective scholarly research dealing with the subject matter of the transcripts
    b. graduate students working on a thesis topic dealing with the subject matter of the transcripts and working under academic supervision

2. Requests for use of the material shall be made in the following way:

    a. the individual will fill out the applicable parts of the "Oral History Interview Form"
    b. graduate students additionally shall present a letter from their supervisory professor, indicating the need to use the material and the nature of the thesis topic
    c. all persons shall execute the "Oral History Transcript Use Contract"

3. Use of the transcript material shall be limited in the following way:

    a. no individual shall remove the transcript from the library
    b. the transcripts shall not be microfilmed or reprinted
    c. the transcripts are not available for inter-library loan
    d. all users of this material shall agree in writing to abide by the above regulations by executing the "Oral History Transcript Use Contract"

4. Procedures on using quotations from transcripts:

    a. if an excerpt or quotation from the transcripts is to be published, the author must submit the name and address of the publisher so that the latter can be informed of the possibility of libelous statements in the transcripts. This is a condition stipulated in the "Oral History Transcript Use Contract" and required of all users.

Oral History Interview Form

Request to use Interviews and Archival Materials

Date ______________________

Name ____

Local Address ______________________ Tel. ____________

Permanent Address ____________________ Tel. ____________

Name of institution with which you are associated ____________

____

Your position in this institution ______________________

University degrees (Name of University, degree, date conferred)

____

____

For what purpose do you wish to use the materials? ____________

____

Name and address of person recommending you ____________

____

Permission is granted to use the following restricted materials:

1. ______________________ 8. ______________________

2. ______________________ 9. ______________________

3. ______________________ 10. ______________________

4. ______________________ 11. ______________________

5. ______________________ 12. ______________________

6. ______________________ 13. ______________________

7. ______________________ 14. ______________________

Additional restrictions: ________________________________

____

____

Date ______________________

Oral History Transcript Use Contract

I, the undersigned, have read the attached document entitled "Archives Handling of Oral History Transcripts" and agree to abide by the rules set down herein and whatever restrictions may have been imposed upon the use of the transcripts.

I affirm that the information that I have provided on the "Oral History Interview Form" is accurate and that it is my intention to use the Oral History transcripts for objective scholarly research.

I acknowledge that I have been warned that the use of libelous statements or the invasions of personal privacy is actionable and may result in sizable damage payments by the parties involved.

I also acknowledge having been warned that slander, i.e., the oral transmission of defamatory statements, is actionable.

I agree that prior to publication of any excerpt or quotation from the Oral History transcripts, I will submit to the Archivist in charge of the materials the name and address of the person or company that plans on printing the material.

____
date

____________________ ____________________
Archivist's signature signed

Rules For Use of Manuscripts in the Michigan Historical Collections of the University of Michigan

1. All materials are to be used in the Michigan Historical Collections.

2. All notes must be taken with pencil or typewriter.

3. The exact order and arrangement of the papers must be kept intact. If any mistake in arrangement is discovered, please call it to the attention of the research assistant. Do not rearrange papers yourself.

4. In citing these materials, cite full name of this depository. Example: Roy D. Chapin Papers, Michigan Historical Collections, The University of Michigan.

5. Microfilming and duplication of records: Because of limited staff facilities, only a very modest amount of copying can be permitted at this time.

    a. Only positive microfilm, photostat or Xerox will be furnished at researcher's expense; these copies are supplied as a temporary loan and must be returned to the Michigan Historical Collections.

    b. No incoming correspondence found in the collection of a contemporary* person can be photoduplicated without the written consent of the writer of these letters or his heirs.

    c. In the James B. Angell Papers, Arthur J. Tuttle Papers, Frank Murphy Papers, Chase S. Osborn Papers, and others designated by the Director, no materials from the non-chronologically arranged special files may be photoduplicated.

6. Securing permission to publish material is the responsibility of the researcher.

*Contemporary is defined as any person whose career extended past 1915.

Registration No. __________

The Library of Congress

Reader's Registration Form For Use of Rare Materials
(The information supplied will be held in confidence)

(To b filled out by hand, in ink, by the reader)

Date ____________________

Name (in full) ____

Home address ____

Washington address __________________________ Telephone ________

Name and address of institution, or organization of affiliation ____

____

Title ____

If a student, indicate degree sought and faculty member directing research ____

Letters of introduction from ____________________________________

____

Other identification submitted __________________________________

____

Principal materials desired ____________________________________

____

Purpose for which materials are requested ______________________

____

Publication plans ____

____

Estimated length of visit ______________________________________

____
(signature of reader)

Interviewed by ____________________
(signature of officer)

Request approved by ____________________
(signature of officer)

(over)

Reader's Agreement to Comply With Rules For Use of Rare Materials in the Library of Congress

The Reader using rare materials is requested to:

1. Deposit his coat, hat, or other personal property not essential to his work, at the check stand at the entrance to the building, or at the place designated for this purpose within the division.
2. Sign the Readers' Register daily.
3. Handle materials only at assigned place.
4. Use no ink, except in ballpoint pens.
5. Limit use of items to the minimum essential to immediate research needs.
6. Make no marks on the materials, write no notes on top of materials, rest no books or other objects on the face or surface of items used, and handle loose sheets or book pages by their edges, avoiding so far as possible touching the surface with the hands.
7. Exercise greatest possible care to prevent damage to materials and extreme care in handling fragile items.
8. Preserve the existing order and arrangement of unbound materials, and report any disarrangement to the attendant in charge.
9. Arrange with the assistant in charge of the reading room (if it is necessary to leave the room temporarily) either to reserve the material for his return or to leave the material on his table provided that he (a) replaces all materials having containers into their proper place, (b) closes all containers and volumes, and (c) notifies the attendant immediately upon his return to resume use of the materials.
10. Return all materials to the issue desk before leaving room for the day or for an extended period, and request the reservation of material to be used again in the immediate future.
11. Submit for inspection any brief case, typewriter case, or any other parcel, book, notebook or other personal property before removing it from the room.
12. Obtain, before publication of manuscript material in the collections of the Library of Congress, advice as to its availability for publication and relevant application of the common law rights in literary property and the laws of libel.

I have read the above rules and hereby agree to abide by them.

Name: ______________________
(Signature of Reader)

Date: ______________________

Appendix VI

Michigan Historical Collections
New Accession

Date______________________ 19_____

From: ____
name

____
address

____

Through: ____

Received by: _ _ _ _ _ _ _ _ _ _ _ _ _ _ _ _ _

Remarks:

AGREEMENT OF DEPOSIT

____

Between

____

and

The Michigan Historical Collections
of the
University of Michigan

Date____________________

It is agreed that the ___________________________________

____________________________are deposited with the Michigan Historical Collections on the following terms:

1. The ownership of the materials remains with __________

   ____

   They may be recalled from the Michigan Historical Collections only by _________________________________

2. They will be made available for examination subject to the rules of the Michigan Historical Collections. Among these rules are the following:

   A. Materials must be used in the reading room of the Michigan Historical Collections, except as provided in article 1.

   B. Note-taking from these records may be done only in pencil, or by typewriter furnished by the consultant. The use of ink is prohibited.

Observance of the rules is expected in return for the responsibility assumed by the Michigan Historical Collections in taking over and preserving these records.

(Signed)_____________________________
For the Michigan Historical Collections

(Signed)_____________________________

____
Depositor

A list of the individual items deposited is to be attached to this sheet.

Index